Poetry

catch
the magic

Editors:
  *Veda Atchley, Kitty Baier, Alice Gresto,
  Jan Hudson, Veronica Michalowski,
  Fritz von Coelln*

Cover: *Veronica Michalowski*

Photography: *Allan Koven*

Preparation: *Jan Hudson*

California State University, Fullerton
Ruby Gerontology Center-7
Fullerton, California 92834-6870

ISBN 9780974740065

Magic Captured

Back in college as a mature adult,
I was part time student, substitute teacher,
as well as a full time wife and mother of three.
In classes at CSUF for over eight years,
I earned my Bachelor's degree, a Masters,
and credentials in counseling and school psychology.

My Speech teacher, Dr. James Young,
influenced my life as the best professor I ever had.
Imagine my delight, years later, to see
his name associated with Poetry in
OLLI classes available to seniors.

I joined Poetry for Pleasure
and here I am, still enjoying the class.
I read, I write, but most of all I anticipate
the weekly gathering of this group
of bright, creative people.

It is a diverse assembly, and yet
we are a loving, cohesive group.
There is talk about what to name our new book
and I vote for "Catch the Magic" because
that is what makes this all so special...
I, for one, have indeed, caught some magic!

-Kitty Baier

First Day

French was a bust.
All those people had taken it
in high school and/or college.
I couldn't even say *Voila* correctly.
Who knew you pronounce it Wah la!

Then I tried Poetry for Pleasure.
As an English major I studied
Shakespeare, Chaucer, Amy Lowell
Browning and Emily Dickinson.
What would this be?

Room 21 was filling quickly.
Peggy Francis greeted me at the door.
I took a seat next to a silver haired lady
with a calm, patient countenance
confident yet serene.
Her name was Ellie.

There was no text cited in the Blue Book
yet, everyone had books or binders.
I had a few of my poems
stuffed in my pocket.

The reading began.
Wow! I'd never heard of these poets.
Who is Mary Oliver?
A poet named Billy Collins?
That sounded like a sidekick
with the Jesse James gang.

There was Ted, reading low and slow
in his droll wisdom and Jim,
with dramatic cadence and pause,
and Jerry, each line a love note to his wife.
Veda danced nude in the moonlight,
Ingrid gave us bewildered questions,
Lorna, her log cabin lines and Fritz,
the revealing towel.

I read my poem and felt quite at home
with some of the best minds in OLLI.

-Alice Gresto

The Cage of Old Age

How did it happen?
Where have we been?
We didn't see it coming
But AGE, somehow, crept in.

All were lithe and happy
In the Springtime of our years,
Then middle age engulfed us
With children and careers.

The trip's been pretty bumpy.
Experience left scars.
Experience? Our teacher,
And we learned well with ours.

We learned to ask some questions
That we really have to ask
Because there are conditions
Assigned to every task.

How long is this movie?
I need to know.
Better sit on the aisle
'cuz I may have to go.

Will I get a bigger gut
If I drink another beer?
And ask the chef, please,
Are there onions in here?

I'm sure to find my keys
Sooner or later,
But what am I looking for
In the refrigerator?

My hair may be white
And my vision now dim,
but look at my husband—
What happened to him?

Knobby fingers, aching toes,
Knees that crackle are my woes.
My hearing is challenged,
And what's more inside…
Cholesterol, triglyceride!

We move a little slower
We sometimes need our pills,
But we've survived deep valleys
And we've climbed rocky hills
To make the world a better place
We do the best we can
To preserve environment
And help our fellow man.

So live, love, laugh,
Remember,
There is life left to live
But it IS December.

OLLI Poetry Class,
April 10, 2013

Illustrations by
Rayleen Williams

CSUF Professor of Management, Emeritus
Chairman of the Board, CSUF Center for Entrepreneurship
Ames helps faculty, students and entrepreneurs to develop their leadership potential, serve their community, and become the best that they can become.   *-Michael D. Ames, Ph. D.*

Two Yellow Roses

Past Christmases' Bloom
Two lives
Interlaced
One

Future Christmases' Bud
A Blessing
Renewed
Joy!

The Parents I Wish I Knew

Where was I born?
I do not know
Perhaps by the side of the road
On a lonely stretch under the stars
Public but private

Who are my parents?
I do not know
Perhaps good people
Perhaps not
One wonders

Love child,
Regretfully given up?
Orphaned by calamity?
Fostered by the State?
Genealogy judicially sealed

Roots deliberately obscured,
I do not lack love.
To those who chose me,
I offer respect and deep appreciation.
Still, I wonder

Who are the parents I wish I knew?
Challenges, opportunities, choices
What would they advise?
I cannot know
Yet, I want to know

My want spurs me on.
Observing, listening, practicing, learning
I choose from the best and build.
The Parents I wish I knew are now within me.
My roots.

Assembled from many greats
Guiding, helping me realize my talents
Buoying my courage
To follow my true calling.
On these roots I stand firm.

The Power of Choice

Why Choice?
God's gift to all?
Is life itself about opportunity,
or heredity and class?
Improvisation or predestination?
Does anybody deserve to win
or lose?
Who makes such choices?
Why do bad things happen to good people,
or good things to bad people?
Who makes such choices?
Where does God reside?
In Nature?
In your mind?
What does God choose?
What do you choose?
Does the universe care?
Or are the forces of nature
powers without choice?
A tumultuous habitat.
A risky home.
Was Nature created by God,
or accepted and respected?
Does it matter?
Nature is our home.
Could we survive without the power of choice?

The Necessity of Strangers

As we approach the close
of the journey that is our lives,
the power of choice still prevails.

We may choose to bar entry
to the new or strange.
Or, we may open our minds and hearts
to now and the future.

And if we choose not to choose?
Motivated by apathy,
indifference,
or fear?
Regardless.
The power of choice still prevails.

Ignoring choice is simply a veiled closing,
of mind,
and heart,
A way of living while already dead.

Aging makes clear the necessity of strangers.
Friends pass away,
as do work, community, and custom.
Our "Known" changes.

The power of choice, and the necessity of strangers
rarely figure into youthful thinking,
about careers,
or dreams of personal success.
Yet choosing to accept the necessity of strangers is key.

Strangers unlock the entry to our minds.
Understanding, caring about strangers,
opens us to innovation,
creativity,
delivering greater value, and
making a powerful difference with whatever we choose to do.

Those who choose to close mind and heart often declare:
We know best.
There is one best way.
Immediate results must be top priority.
Our competitive edge is having the right expertise.
Only ideas from within our circle are valuable.
We must protect our knowledge.
Only people we know are important.

Those who chose to open mind and heart speak
differently:
We may not know best.
There are many ways to do things.
Discovering new possibilities must be top priority.
Our competitive edge is openness to change.
Engaging with strangers is the best way to come up with
ideas.
We should share our knowledge.
Strangers are also important.

How will we choose to age?
Will we strive for success,
become both older and wiser, and
die while we are living?
Or will we clutch the past,
reassure ourselves that we know best, and
merely live to become older,
while we are already dead?

Now and in the future,
how will we choose to age?
The power of choice prevails,
and the necessity of strangers is key.

Ready For Success?

Courage and persistence
find pathways
around weakness.
To strength.
To success.

Decide what you would be.
Obstacles?
The root breaks the rock.
Wind and water triumph over stone.
Strive.

Set to it like flowing water,
torrent, quiet stream, or drip.
As needs be.
Always steady.
Unstoppable.

Poetry feeds my soul and everywhere I look I see a poem. I wrote my first one when I was 5 years old. Carl Sandberg said, "Poetry is an echo asking a shadow to dance." Bill Heckman, a poet, a teacher and my friend, once said that he was amazed at all the poems walking around, masquerading as people. I agree! 'Nuff said.   *–Veda Atchley*

Five Again

Life flows fast

Wasn't it only yesterday
   when I stood in our garden
     with my father
       and he plucked
         the first ripe tomato
           and placed it in
             my hand?

"Taste the sun," he said
   and I bit into the
     true red fruit, and
       with juice running down my chin,
         dripping onto
           my pinafore

I smiled
   through the seeds,
     swallowed, and said
       "Now I'm a Sun Princess"

He laughed,
   Tousled my curls
     and the sun warmed my skin
       and my heart felt
         plump and proud

Endings/Beginnings

the wind came first—
stirring me out of a dream
then the rain—cleansing the streets,
the houses, my thoughts,
softening the rough edges

the scattered chirping of birds
brings hope, and spring,
just a leaf or two away,
nudges in, ever new,
filled with offerings

the days keep spreading wider
making room for change:
new ways of seeing
other ways of being
altered directions

possibilities bloom like flowers
on the hot desert floor
surprise us with bursts of color
promising the certainty
of ever-returning spring
Nothing stays exactly the same
new dimensions and subtle shifts
whatever our heartbeat envisions
The world is a canvas—

Pick up your paintbrush!

Early June

It is the time of jacarandas
and agapanthus, and
lavender bursts out
all over town

I lean earthwards
yearning to dig deep
in the soil
put in plants
quickly, before spring
runs away

I catch my breath
as I drive down streets
crowded on each side
with tall trunks
and lacey flowering
branches

that reach across the street
to meet cousins
forming a canopy
of purple lace

In front of the little houses
lining the street
purple puddles grow
ever-widening
and renewing
as the branches
sway to the beat
of spring

Celebrating their annual
coming-out party

SEASONING

Winter   Outside—a meadow lark teases
    while the rain,
      in intermittent interludes
      falls softly

From the window, a flock of birds
    aerobatic silhouettes
      gray on gray
      and one—
    sitting on the fence
      breaking his lungs
        to fill the silver hours
          with color
  now gone
  so soon

Spring   Mother Earth, in labor, groans
    toward Spring
between contractions you can
  hear a bird announcing her
    progress and wet your lips
    with showers
      that cool her brow
while the sun skips through
  a field of mustard plants
    preparing a warm
      receiving blanket
      for her new season

Summer   Those Summers!
    opening up their skies
      with warm and
        flowers spilling over—
    green, wrapping around cities
      and meadows
        wild with yellow
    birds weaving silken melodies
      on linen breezes—
    tapestries to hang
      on blue-drenched skies
        while long
          sun-washed days
        stretch out to nap

Autumn A chorus of leaves in scarlet and golden hues
    grace the branches of the trees
    preparing for their final performance
      how they preen
    one by one they curtsey
      leave the stage
        fluttering, floating, falling
          like pages of a book
        toward the inviting earth
they cluster together
    dreaming their long sleep
      in the land of their birth

Written on a Napkin

From the veranda of the
    Hotel Laguna
keeping company with a
    Ramos Fizz—

I spy, beyond the
  sunbathers and the
  volleyball beachers
    a row (more or less)
    of stately (more or less)
palm trees

Well, maybe not stately—
all right! rather scraggly palms
  with long necks and
  shaggy heads
pointing not always straight up

I imagine picking one
  tickling backs, toes,
    tummies of those
  sol-worshipping
    sunbathers
    volley ball beachers

Hilarity ascends from this
  veranda, in this
    beach city as I
  contemplate this
    ticklish delight

  Also—I'd like to take one home

A Hot Fairy Tale

Bronzed and Beautiful
she lays, partner to the sun
wondering, wishing, wanting
always more
soaking up the rays—turning
like a lover to receive blessings
turning her body as on a rotisserie
all evenly tanned, she revels
reflecting old Sol, her lover,
intimately touching her,
day after day

The summer days are long—
many rays penetrate her body
she wears the gift proudly
delights in the pursuant envy,
forgoing future worries,
warnings by doctors

Smitten, she lays, opening herself
giving of herself, letting
Sol have his way with her
carrying his warmth
showing off his gifts

An ardent pursuer, he
assures her she will be envied
fickle lover that he is—
he ignores the future .
this love is for the day—
this day, right now
and he gives his all to her
as she gives back her body

Their affair continues
as long as she offers
herself to him
she thinks she is his only lover
but even if there were more—
she knows he loves her best
she is the chosen one
never, never will he desert her

And so on and so on and so on
you know the unhappy ending
to this story.

An Early Morning Musing

What makes a poem?
 A hunger
 A wish
 A want
Hoping to fulfill all three

Knowing it's tenuous
Nothing is promised
Noting the vacancy
Around you
Yet full to bursting
With possibilities in your wake
The joy of hope
Each morning

At night
When stars litter the sky
Or the moon, big pearl
Dominates the dark
When doubts arise
Reclaim their thrones

And you—
Wonder-filled, with angst
Retreat to memories
Re-walk paths
Re-live past loves
Explore their virtues
Discard their deceptions
Embrace the little deaths
Extol the morrows

Still—with
 That hunger
 That wish
 That want

I've changed:
from short and kinda cute to short and
kinda fat -from a "brownette" to silver
hair, and while I still have good legs,
I'm wrinkled.
All through early education, I was
youngest in my classes. Now I am
often the oldest ... but it does
not matter. I enjoy laughter, singing, dancing and writing and I can
continue all of those things in this fun program called OLLI.

-Kitty Baier

How To Write a Poem

Poems need not rhyme -
so start with a simple sentence
but spread it over several lines.
See how easy that is?

Try to be lyrical.
Poems should contain detail
but avoid being contrived
or dogmatic.
Those mistakes spoil your work.

Words like "very", "really", "stuff" and "things"
add little
but might be inserted
to smooth the meter.

Usually, one should be grammatically correct,
but while my poem "Top Priority" that follows
should read "It is I"
I changed to "it's only me...."
because that's the way I speak—

Your rapt attention I now seek:
Not just today, but all next week.
Each poem written is unique
but be on guard for tongue in cheek.

Top Priority

Do you ever get the feeling that someone is watching?
Well, it's only me ...
because I care deeply and want to be sure
you are OK.
I will stand in the way of any problem that I see
because I want to shield you
from hurt, insult or physical harm.

I am not the brightest person you know,
nor the most resourceful.
I am not physically robust,
I carry no weight socially,
know no one influential,
but if LOVE counts at all
I've got your back.

You need not share confidences
nor even call.
Just know that if I can help
I'll be there physically,
emotionally, financially,
and with my prayers.

I hope you have felt me
cheering you on
as an encouraging onlooker,
and when you've stumbled
or tumbled,
you've found my arms
a soft place to fall.

I have many responsibilities—
some I assumed voluntarily,
others were caused by circumstance,
but my job
as loving parent and friend
has always
taken top priority!
Please know how dear you are to me.

Times Change

I scan
the back to school ads ...
A bedspread, that matches the drapes,
as well as the towels and the hamper.
There's also a bulletin board and a waste basket.
Even the photo frame and a water bottle blend in—
all color coordinated.

I remember
my trip to the University of Minnesota.
I was not yet seventeen,
was anticipating a job in the dorm
as I rode the train overnight to "The Cities",
carrying a battered suitcase with tape on the corners
and a cardboard box tied with clothesline.

Nothing matched
nothing blended
all things patched
but neatly mended.

I recall an old army blanket
that was scratchy and UGLY
but warm on cold winter nights.
I carried a few articles of clothing
and wore a coat
but I did not even own an alarm clock.

Those were days with zero dollars.
Frugal days of care.
People talk of "the good ole days"...
    but I had pins in my underwear.

I don't ever want to be so poor again!

Remember To Remember

I've reached an age when memory can fade.
When one cannot recall events
that made their life unique.
How awful that must be.

I understand not being sure
about some neighbor's name
or what happened on a date
long in the past.

But a few even forget their own children.
How could that be?
Family is so important.
I hope that never happens to me.

Some must see a total blank.
It's as though some events never happened.
It must be like turning on the slide projector
but seeing only darkness.

I am aware that some activities
that I recall a certain way
are remembered differently by others
even though we shared the same experience.

I realize that not all memories are happy ones.
Sometimes failures or embarrassing moments
stand out more than our successes.
But to have learned nothing
from our mistakes in life .... How sad!

And so I am beginning
an autobiography of sorts.
Trying to write down what happened,
where I was, who I was with,
 how I felt and what I learned.

It doesn't matter that events were ordinary,
that my life was unexciting when compared to others.
What I will record will be how I felt about my time on earth.
Then, maybe, as I grow even older
and need reminders
I can read my own words to jog my memory.

What Friendship Means

Friendship is a bank account made out in your name
for you to draw upon to fill your needs ...
whether your desires are material things or service deeds.
It's like the treasury of unconditional love I offer to my
children;
like the love I had for my husband: a limitless supply of
giving.

It could be a simple favor, or moral support,
genuine empathy in times of trouble ... and TOUCH
whether that means a pat on the back, or a hug,
a helping hand, a swat on the fanny,
or a kick in the ass.   I touch.

With my family there has been no keeping score
of what was done for whom.
I chose an outstanding father for my kids.
Now needs are met as they arise
and I hope there is enough for everyone.
I wish I could offer more financial help to grandchildren
because they need money for college,
but I know some struggle will serve to build their strength.

So you may dip into the friendship fountain
at any time and use whatever I can supply.
Might as well, my friend, because
it sure looks like you are stuck with me!

Faith Can Be Fragile

When things go smoothly in our lives
we credit ourselves.
After all, we had good intentions,
we worked hard, and so, deserve success!
But we should be glorifying God.

When our daily lives are only so-so,
we promise to put in more effort
but we grumble and complain.
We blame bad timing or bad luck.
We need to practice patience.

In times of trouble we seek religion,
so we ask for divine guidance...
but usually what we really want
is God's interference with the Laws of Nature
that He so meticulously created.

When there is deep distress, nearly everyone
wants to believe that there is a Super Power
that can intervene in some way
to ease the suffering of a loved one.
It is then that we fall on our knees.

Man is so self-centered, so vain,
so demanding, so hedonistic, that
Our Creator must feel tremendous disappointment
unless, (just consider this idea)
we were created for His amusement.

That would explain the random acts of violence,
disease, pestilence, famines, floods and wars.
What if God is just relaxing on some cloud
while this little game called "The Human Race" goes on?
Faith can be a fragile thing.

May Faith Be Strong!

The professionals who deal with STRESS
Know that FAITH is powerful
As an antidote for the poisons
That DOUBT and HERESY can cause.

With FAITH comes HOPE
The ability to look for rainbows
Even during the fiercest storm-
The proverbial light at the end of the tunnel,
With every glass half full.

FAITH leads to TRUST
And opens the door to APPRECIATION
Of all the WONDERS of this earth
And its place in time and space.

FAITH encourages LOVE, COMPASSION for others
And EMPATHY for those with problems.
It helps to HEAL and maintain MENTAL HEALTH.
FAITH is in the essence of the HOLY SPIRIT.
It is a GIFT from GOD.

He Still Winked At Me

He didn't say "I love you" everyday
nor did I whisper those words to him,
but we SHOWED that we loved one another
well into our sixth decade together.
We had a division of duties, but
he helped with the housework
so he ran the washing machine
and the vacuum as often as I did.
The cars were his domain so they
and the garden were well maintained.
I handled the finances and the children,
but knew I had an assistant, if needed.
I KNOW and appreciate how LUCKY I was!

A smile, a wink or a touch
was all that was needed to convey
affection, respect and concern.
We traveled, we fished, we danced,
we entertained. We had fun together,
and he was "The Best Dad Ever!"
Those are the words the kids put
on his headstone at the cemetery.
I don't want that changed
when I join him there.

But I am still here and
able to work to help others.
I pray for the health, the energy, the joy
to do good things with the time that remains.
Each morning I brush my attitude
to begin the adventures of another day,
knowing that a wonderful man,
a really cute old guy
still winked at me!

Edith Bockian

While I was four, my mother polished her English attending a local class. I'd sit beside her in the evening, when she did her homework. As a result, I learned to read and enjoyed playing a game of rhyming words on paper she provided. Writing my own verses was an easy step from then on. WW II found me including poems in daily letters to my husband (in the Philippines) to fill up space when there was nothing new to add. During my teaching years, I'd write personal poems for students as an incentive for them to improve their reading skills. And, then came OLLI - to my delight, encouraging my poetic efforts further.

-Edith Bockian

Advice Comes

Advice comes
    Abundant, spilling over,
    Offered, as fruit in season,
    To all within reach:

    The saturated as well as the famished,
    The curious, the indifferent,
    The hostile, the allergic,
    The wounded, the unneeding.

Reach cautiously,
    Turn the offerings around and 'round,
    Underneath it all there may be rot,
    The hole through which the worm has
    wound his way.

    Yet some are worthy of an instant bite,
    A perfect ripeness born of love—or thought—
    Or knowledge - fed by open air and light.

    Choose, if you will, to pass unseeing,
    Or pocket what you will for later use,
    Or, all signs being favorable,
    Savor what is served
    And satisfy the void.

Advice comes.

Tomorrows Soon Are Yesterdays

(Thoughts on My 75th Year)

It's been a long journey—
Partly planned, partly stumbled upon,
But always advancing—
How soon it seems tomorrows
Become my yesterdays !

Time to reflect upon life's winding down.
 It's been a mixed bag
        Pluses and minuses
        Assets and liabilities
        Ups and downs.

In retrospect, would I repeat
All that has gone before?
Am I now so steeped in wisdom
I could plot an idyllic path?

Suffice it to say I did
What I thought best
With the knowledge then at hand—
Trying hard, balancing needs...
Yet... I am left with wondering
In times of quiet contemplation
Had I changed the written page
Could I have done more?

No matter. For now I note
With softly indrawn breath
Days trip over days that hurry by
Hurtling toward an unseen finish line.
Too soon, it seems, tomorrows
Become my yesterdays.

Remembering

Another year is coming to a close—
And though, with wisdom, we should plan ahead
I'll follow back to where my mem'ry flows,
Revisit journeys we have made, instead.

Together, armed with film and maps galore,
We wheeled across the country, east and west,
And picked some wondrous places to explore,
We thought the red rock country was the best.

Once tribes of Indian natives shared their wealth
Of handsome pottery and turquoise jewels,
Once we descended down a canyon steep,
Riding on the backs of skillful mules.

Remember stalactites and stalagmites?
We inched down ladders for that awesome sight,
When we emerged it was a thrill to see
The cave bats fly across the moon at night.

There were the forests, lush and vast and still,
So many rivers, lakes and waterfalls,
And skies of such a splendid, intense blue.
There's more this fading memory recalls.

Like waking to snow covered cars in June
When visiting the mighty Yellowstone,
But geysers, herds of bison and of elk,
Make this a memory I gladly own.

You've helped to make those images, and more,
So, let the clock tick on and time go by,
Although our wheels no longer tour the land,
We're memory rich forever, you and I.

Family Reunion

While the women moved the after-dinner dishes
From table to sink, with clatter and chatter,
And assorted uncles and cousins
Grouped to talk of politics, and the cost of living,
The girls sprawled on the rug, giggling
And ah-h-ing at some new found treasure.
David, having had his fill of terrier-teasing,
Ambled over nonchalantly to see
What he might be missing.

"It's Grandma's photo album," Jenny volunteered.
Prominent upon the page, on a print, brown-toned,
A straight backed, mustached fellow stared ahead,
Hand upon a table, as if to steady himself before
The slow recording eye of an ancient camera.

"I think he was a colonel in the Civil War,"
She crowed. "Wish we could trace our family
To the Revolution. Know a girl at school who can,
And is she ever proud!"

David shrugged, remembering Paul,
The greatest friend a guy could ever have.
He could only trace his ancestors
To Auschwitz.

Nostalgia

It seemed like such a perfect way
To flee the city's summer heat—
A few hour's drive.
Our destination, some retreat
We used to visit faithfully
Come each July, when I was young.
Gladly would I change these concrete miles
For those meadows filled with daisies
And buttercups and thistle,
For those unobtrusive mountain roads
Guarded by tiger-lilies,
Embroidered with Queen Anne's lace,
For the cool tree-lined lake
Approached through a cornfield
And over the railroad track.

We found it in the afternoon,
New widened roads had sped us on.
Parked, we stared and shook our heads.
The summer cottage in a flowered meadow
Had shrunk in disrepair in a weed patch
Like old jeans emerging from a dryer,
Ragged, faded, two sizes smaller.
The lake, a moment away,
Was but a mud hole.

Some jester, some practical joker,
Some mad and mocking magician,
Must have ached with riotous laughter
As we eagerly reached for a gemstone
And pulled out a shriveled walnut.

Magic

Somehow you always knew
When I was harried
Rattled, at loose ends,
What special magic
Lulled and calmed and soothed.

Not pills, nor words—
You'd open up your arms
And let me in
And close them 'round me
Gentle, firm, secure.

A moment thus, and with
A shuddered sigh
Whatever were the cares,
Fancied or real,
Would drop away and leave me
Free, refreshed
Ready to do battle.

Somehow you always knew—
When I was harried,
Rattled, at loose ends.

Mothers Say (To my Son at Sixteen)

Mothers say
> My how you've grown
> It seems like almost yesterday
> Pink faced, hungry,
> We brought you home,
> A complaining bundle.

Mothers say all this
And I am no exception.
> We brought you home
> Nourished you with
> Nutriments and affection,
> Watched you blossom
It's awesome observing
> A youngster grow
> Mastering activity after
> Complex activity.
It's awesome, peering upon
> The relaxed beauty
> Of a sleeping child
> Knowing you've played a small part
> In this amazing achievement.

And the tendency
> Is to want to protect
> This near perfect creation
> From day to day.
> Keep it safe, unspoiled
> From the known and unknown terrors
> Of Out There.

But, now
I tip my head
To see the crest of yours.
The last of the strings
Will soon be severed
As surely as was
That umbilical
To give you life apart.
Then will you decide all
Your entrances and exits
While, like mothers everywhere,
I will hover nervously
In the wings

What Is a Poem

A poem is an art form—
Words are its brush strokes—
Its colors, its patterns—
With lines that fill the eyes and ears,
Penetrate the mind, the heart—
Liberating, at last, the poet
With thoughts that must be said.

Marsha Chotiner

I was born and raised in Los Angeles. Thirty-seven years ago, my husband of almost 50 years and our children moved to La Mirada. For many years, I was extremely active in fundraising for the benefit of children, raising my family and supporting my husband's efforts on the La Mirada City Council.

 When my children were both in school full time I went back to work for the Norwalk La Mirada Unified School District as a Children's Librarian in both the elementary and middle school levels. There was not a day that went by that I didn't look forward to opening the library, having the room filled with students and helping them find "The Right Book."

In my decision to retire, I was concerned about what would fill my days and how I would continue to learn and be challenged. It was that year that my friend, Juanita Driskell invited me to an OLLI Open House suggesting that I might enjoy "Poetry for Pleasure."

For 31 years, as a Children's Librarian, I was always surrounded by works of many authors.

Little did I know that I would continue to be surrounded by works of many authors only this time the authors would be the members of "Poetry for Pleasure."

How lucky can one person be!   -Marsha Chotiner

I'M A WOMAN

W-O-M-A-N

Hear me roar.

Nothing nor no one can stop me from achieving more.

'Cause I'm a Woman

W-O-M-A-N

Career, Motherhood, Wife and Friend,

I have always had the ability to bend.

'Cause I'm a Woman

W-O-M-A-N

Overcoming obstacles, a life filled with joy and sorrow,

I wake each morning filled with love and hope and never
worry about tomorrow.

'Cause I'm a Woman

W-O-M-A-N

You Bet I Am

So Much Better Than Being a Man!

(Inspired by Peggy Lees rendition)

Longing To Hear His Voice

Sitting by the fountain in my garden with the morning
frost on the ground, I try to be as quiet as possible.

Longing to Hear His Voice.
They tell me it will happen if only I let it.

The scent on his clothes has faded away.
The sound of his voice has faded away.

But, I know, if I hear his voice just one more time maybe
the suffering will ease just a little.

Longing to Hear His Voice.
They tell me it will happen if only I let it.

I try to be patient and clear my mind, when all of a
sudden there is a whispering sound.

Looking up, I notice the trees rustling in the wind.

We Are Not Getting Another Dog

We are not getting another dog

We are travelers now, free spirits.

No more commitments or responsibilities.

We are travelers now, free spirits.

What! You say she was on the streets for weeks,
pregnant, lost all her puppies and up for adoption.

How sad, but we are not getting another dog.

You asked if we wanted to hold her.

We said, "No Thanks."

You asked if we wanted to take her for a little walk.

We said, "No Thanks."

You see, we are not getting another dog.

We are travelers now, free spirits

We named her "Maddie" and when asked what breed she
is, our answer is, "Brown and Tan."

We got another dog.

We still are travelers and free spirits but now there are
three of us.

I guess you could call me a late bloomer. I married at age thirty-two, received a B.A. in English from Cal State Fullerton in 1976 at age forty-four. I have five grandchildren, oldest one 12, so you can see my children followed suit, having their children when they were over thirty. I have been a poet since I was in grade school, but this is my first time to be published. I hope to  publish my first fiction book for middle grade children this year; then I will be an author! This is my second year at OLLI and my favorite class by far is Poetry for Pleasure.   *-Barbara de Best*

The Library Cat
(Trapped behind the library)

I have a cat that lives under my bed.
It's hard to tell if it's living or dead.
The problem is this: I can't get it out;
To get under beds I'm rather too stout.
I call it "Domino"—it's black and white.
What good is a name if it's never in sight?
It just comes out when there's no one around
And it skitters back under at the first sound.
I know, because the litter box fills;
The food dish empties; the water cup spills.
But worst of all is when it's in season.
It yowls and complains way beyond reason.
My dog goes crazy; my other cat's nutty.
They're not used to a cat that is slutty.
I'll trap it, I'll fix it, and then what to do?
Is there a place for a cat at the zoo?
But seriously, though, I could let it outside;
It won't have kittens, and won't have to hide.
But there are lots of dangers outside to dread,
So I think I'll keep it safe under my bed.

Russia 1992

I wish you had been with me in Russia
Seen the colorful fairy tale churches
Symbolic of a former life.
And dwellings of a Stalin gray
Reminders of the tyrant's sway.

In the quiet of Red Square
We imagine ghosts of Cossacks
Riding with their flashing swords
Past St. Basil's and along the Kremlin wall
Where their smitten enemies did fall.

We would almost hear the hoof beats
See the icy clouds of steam
From the horses' flaring nostrils
Galloping through the mists of ages
Settling into history's pages.

We would stand at Lenin's tomb
Which lies in state within the Kremlin walls
Seen now only by the curious
Where unfurrowed in the waxen brow.
Safe from worms, at least for now.

In the Square there is no place to rest
Even in St. Basil's people stand
For hours on end to worship God
Coming out of hiding now at last
Trying to rekindle what was past.

We would go to the circus, laugh and clap
Until the clumsy bear began to dance
We wonder, did the laughing people know
That bears like these danced for the czar?
Do they now think back that far?

Then we would walk down streets of gray
Where citizens lived in cell-like rooms
And children gray as cloudy skies
Played in narrow alleyways
Between those gray buildings of the Stalin days.

So we would seek a happier place
Looking for Moscow in the theater where
Upon the stage the dancers whirled
In many-colored clothes that showed their wear
And yet they spun and twirled without a care.

We would walk among the hucksters in the streets
Selling painted dolls and other souvenirs
And we would buy, because both they and beggars
Looked alike in dignity and stance
And in their faces hope asked for a chance.

In concert halls we heard the Russian soul:
Their music which has struggled to be free
Melodies that came from imprisoned hearts
Music wrought from suffering and pain
From a land that sang and wrote while held in chains.

And we would ask ourselves again,
Where is the real Russia that we seek?
Is it the penetrating grayness of the land
Or the melancholy loneliness of prayer
Or the palpable presence of despair?

These people are the remnants of a war
That took a generation from the land
Where twenty-five million people died
And graves were marked not with names but years
And hard-won victory caused wives and children tears.

But our time in Moscow would not give up
Its secrets anymore than the endless graves
Will give up the multitudes who died
Because they loved their Motherland
And suffered like all who make a stand.

Mistress Black Widow

I'm Mistress Black Widow; I live in a shed.
I'm usually widowed right after I'm wed.
When people come in they leave with a shout.
They slam the door shut; they're glad to get out.
"There's a spider in there all shiny and black!
It has a red spot tattooed on its back."

I'm so insulted because they should see
It's not on my back; it's on my tummy.
It's not a spot; it's an hourglass shape.
Please come closer; don't stand there and gape.

I've had many husbands; I get such a thrill;
I don't kiss and tell—I kiss and kill.
But I always set the young ones free;
So I guess you might say I commit bigamy.
There are many tasties on my table for one:
Flies, moths, mosquitoes and beetles are fun.

As to why I bite people like you I must say
It's merely because you get in my way.

Travel Journals In Verse

China 2008

I came expecting to respect your people
To stand in awe before the precious treasures:
The Great Wall and the terra cotta warriors
To hear stories of ancient dynasties
To see the new world you are starting to become.
All of this I did expect and did enjoy.
But when I saw the delicate embroidery
And the exotic patterns of the cloisonné
The soft and flowing harvest of the silkworm
Jade in hues the rainbow never knew
All created by the patience of the craftsmen
All bespoke of artist and the poet.
I sensed in this the spirit of your people
That could not be destroyed by emperors' edicts
That could not be defeated by Mao's directives.
There exists a celebration of life
Of beauty in all elements of nature
Translated into creations of the heart.
China, I did not know that I would love you
I did not expect a glimpse into your soul.

Tanzania 2004

I sing the song of the Serengeti
Of Arusha and Tarangire
Of Kilimanjaro and Mt. Meru
Of skies of gray and skies of blue

The clouds uncountable on high
Uncountable antelope passing by
We slept in lodges brimming with bloom
And walk-in tents with lots of room

Maasai men wear garments of red
Women carry baskets of food on their head
One morning on a walk with our group
Our guide expounded on elephant poop.

Millions and millions of years ago
A volcano collapsed in Ngorongoro
Leaving a caldera twelve miles wide
Where thousands of animals live inside

Wildebeests with the Zebras stay
Trying to avoid being lion prey
The wildebeest, being not so bright,
Depends on the zebra to announce the flight

No rain 'til October is the rule
But September rains make a wallowing pool
The clouds explode and drench the earth
Cooling the air and settling the dirt.

All of our guides showed us the way
To the predators and their prey
Bumping and jostling on long, dirt covered roads
We saw gazelle and impala of which there were loads.

It is a fierce land of hunting and killing
Of vultures picking, their bellies filling
With shreds of bloated buffalo meat
Which to a vulture are quite a treat.

In a huge balloon up in the sky
Some of us were seen gliding by
Then, underneath the acacia tree,
Like the English, we sipped our tea.

Leopard, we heard you, and in a tree, saw your kill
But for seeing you, do you think we will?
A rogue elephant tried to attack our car
Chased it, but not very far.

The croc's a prehistoric sight
The hippo—there's nothing like his bite.
The ubiquitous hyena's call
Kept us awake and disturbed us all.

On our last night at camp close to view
Eight young lions paraded through.
They did not look from left to right
But still they gave us quite a fright.

The sounds of silence, of animals too
How do we leave Africa? It's hard to do.

The Park
(Circa 1937)

The park—endlessly green, huge, limitless
To me at five or six,
Steel-tubed galactic universe of play
We glided on the horizontal swinging board
We called "the boat."
And from the dizzying top
We took a final step onto a slick
And shiny slide
And with swift sucking-in of breath
Took the downward plunge
Into the sand.

The jungle gym was where we twisted in and out through
A crisscross steel maze of tubes,
Legs up, head dangling, laughing at
Our funny faces upside down and streaming hair

The double swing pumped by four of us
Swinging into the very sky it seemed
The teeter-totter with its up and down jolt would
Set our teeth on edge.
The water from the fountain that gushed
Into our noses made us cough and laugh.

The picnics—best of all—bringing
Raging appetites to a red-checkered tablecloth feast.
The cloth held down by sandwiches and potato salad.
And the banquet bliss of chips and soda pop.
The smoky smell of burgers, hot dogs, and toasted buns,
My mother fanning away the flies.
Finally, a nickel run to the
Ice cream stand for cones
That melted faster than we could lick them up
And in the background, horseshoes
Clinking against the poles
Accompanied by the deep laughter of my dad,
His gold tooth flashing in the summer sun.

December (Full Moon)

The sun licks at the rim of the world
With fiery tongue
Its twilight mouth a blur of orange
Lilac and gray
The yawn of the approaching night
Smears the color palette of the sun.
The moon arises full and bright
And casts a spell of daylight on the snow.

I entered the poetry haven of Room 21 seven years ago just to see what it was like after being invited by a member of the class who said it was a fun place to be. Boy, was she ever right!! I have been there ever since, every Thursday, with my poems to share. I have actually even written some poems of my own, some of which are included here. It certainly is different being on this side of the desk after 31 years at the front of the classroom as the teacher, but I can say that I have found a new "family" of friends here because we have shared so much together. If any of you get the chance to join us, please do—you'll find it's fun, just as I did.   *-Juanita Driskell*

In The Garden

The fountain burbled a concerto in the garden
as the cat delicately picked her way along the ground.
She needed to hurry
before the frost embroidered patterns
on the walkways and grass
made it hard on her paws.
She was an indoor cat normally,
but a strange and exotic scent had drawn her outdoors.

As she followed her nose,
she stopped upon hearing whisperings
breaking the silence
as if someone were telling secrets.
When the quiet resumed,
she sauntered on
still intent on this new fragrance
invading her world.

Suddenly, there it was,
the smell so strong
it almost put her into a stupor.
She had fallen into the garlic patch
and was now suffering from an overdose
of too much smell.
And there were the whisperings again!

It was definitely time to get back inside
for a good bath and a warm fire.

Hey, I'm An Old Lady

Hey, I'm an old lady!
When did this happen?
I've been monitoring every morning,
and the face that greets me each day,
seems the same as when I was 18.

I am perplexed
because most days
I don't feel old.
I still feel as if I could go out
and conquer the world.
Bring it on!

Though lately,
I can feel the old lady's
icy fingers on my neck,
a lot!

What happened?
Is it because I slept in this morning
and missed the cut-off date
for being young?

It just can't be
because when I was 18,
I was sure I wouldn't live past 40
because 40 was grotesquely old.

And yet some of the best things in my life
happened past the age of 40.
How ironic is that?

I think it's still a state of mind,
and never mind what the mirror
or the aches and pains in my body say.
I could go out and conquer the world,
but first
I have to go take a nap!

Takers

Takers, grabbers, moochers,
sleaze balls, shirkers, welfare queens.
Are there any other pejoratives to use?
Takers was a popular term
used during the last election cycle
and is still running around out there.

It is so easy to label those
who are different from us,
people who have less than us.
And aren't we lucky that we have more,
that we have as much as we have?

But to label people in this way
is to begin not
to understand their plight,
to not walk a while in their shoes.

Perhaps we've been lucky enough
not to have to apply for welfare,
or have to accept food stamps,
or help from WIC
just in order to survive.
And lucky we are!

But to feel resentment and anger for people
less fortunate than we
is to deny God's principles and love.

If the non-takers had their way,
they would not want any takers.
Does that mean that the takers
and their children
would all be out on the street
starving to death?
Or maybe they'd all be
in debtors' prison
as in Dickensian times.

Or perhaps we'd actually raise the minimum wage
and cut out tax loopholes for the wealthy
so it would be a more level playing field.
Now wouldn't that be something!

In the meantime,
perhaps we could just feel
a little more charitable
for the less fortunate among us.

Please!

Daddy

It was always Daddy,
not Dad, or Father, or Pop,
but Daddy.
You held us together after Mommy died,
as much holding as there could be,
and sometimes it seemed like not enough.

Did you know that the best times
were the times it was just
you, me, and Rita?
When you made your famous slumgullion,
or even when you made those hideous drinks
after you bought the blender at the county fair.
Rita and I learned to run
when you dragged out the blender
and all the green ingredients.
I can still see you pursuing us
through the house to the front door
with the glass of green glop in your hand.

But you got lonely and then searched for a new mate,
one to possibly be a new mother to us as well.
So there was Gladys, and Betty, and Dorothy.
Dorothy, a name that still brings me chills.
When Dorothy decided Rita and I
were a burden she did not want,
the plan was hatched
to dump us in Milwaukee
with your mother.
But you didn't go through with it.
Was it because you would miss us too much,
or was it simply a matter of the cost?
I'd like to think it was the act of missing us,
but maybe I'm being an optimist.

You were a difficult man to know,
one who found it hard to admit affection,
who never said "I love you".
But I knew and felt your love,
though it took me a while to perceive it
as I grew up and away.

I am sorry for the end of your life
spent alone.
But it was you who chased people away,
too proud to admit you needed love too.
I felt guilty for not letting you live with us,
but I didn't think I could trust how
you would act around a 12 year old girl,
and I didn't want to take that chance.

I loved you with all of my heart
and forgave you always!

Malala's Dream

There are different acts of bravery,
and there are different dreams.
Malala Yousafzai's dream was simple:
she just wanted an education.
A simple dream, maybe,
especially in this day and age.
But Malala had the misfortune
of living in a country sometimes
overrun by the Taliban.
And the Taliban has decreed
that education is not a good thing,
and most especially not a good thing
for girls.
After all, a girl needs only to know
how to cook for her husband
and spread her legs for him on demand.

But Malala wasn't to be bowed down,
so she started speaking out
against this injustice when she was only eleven.
She continued to want to go to school,
even when the Taliban not only closed schools,
but blew them up!

So, did it take an act of bravery
for her to continue going to school?
Did it take an act of bravery for a Talib,
dressed in his beard
and dreams of virgins in heaven,
to shoot her and two other girls
as they rode home from school?
He certainly thought so!

But it turned out that shooting Malala
didn't kill her
or kill her spirit.
She recovered
and continued to speak out for her dream.
Because of her courage,
and because of her dream
she was honored at the United Nations
on her sixteenth birthday.

Now she is inspiring other young people,
as well as world leaders with the same dream.

And you just want to say,
"Yea, Malala! You go girl!"
Because even if they were to kill you,
your dream would still live on.

Our Lives

The Venetian blinds are slanted up
to keep out the worst of the summer sunlight and heat.
It creates a cozy, intimate atmosphere.
The room is redolent
with the fragrance of Mum deodorant
and my mother's bath soap.

My sister and I lounge on the end of the bed
and watch our mother dress after her shower.
She spreads the deodorant on her underarms,
then places the foam rubber inserts into her bra
and folds her breasts,
depleted after nursing all twelve of her children,
including me, the last of the twelve,
into the cups.

Her life hadn't been depleted with all the kids,
so this is the time she tells us stories of her past life.
She tells of her life with her strict, immigrant, Polish parents,
grandparents I've never met,
and of how they wouldn't let her date until she was eighteen.

She talks about her life with the first husband,
and of how hard it was living with an alcoholic
who she'd say bitterly, "...knew how to do only two things,
drink and piss the bed."
Obviously there was more he knew how to do.
They made ten children together.

She tells of how the kids would bring home
all of the diseases common then,
of whooping cough, scarlet fever, mumps,
diphtheria, and of how one of those kids
had died from diphtheria.

In all of these tellings,
she never once told us of her feelings
and we, being children,
weren't insightful enough to ask.

There may be more that I don't remember now
almost sixty years later.
But they provided a glimpse into my mother,
a woman who was a person before she was "Mommy."

But they are only pieces of her life,
puzzle pieces to fit together as best I can,
and I wish now that she had told more.
I never got to know her as a woman person,
only as Mommy, the mother person.

She meant so much to me
but I have so little
because we had such little time
in our lives together.

A Child's Garden of Verses by Robert Louis Stevenson was the book that introduced Esther to poetry when she was a child. She still cherishes that same book. Esther's first original poem was written in 1953, in honor of President Eisenhower's Inauguration Day. She loves the Poetry for Pleasure class here at OLLI, and she conducts a poetry class at an assisted living facility in Garden Grove. Esther has been married to Bob for 48 years, and they have two adult sons.

–Esther Fieldhouse

Bagpipes

It's an instrument with a story that often has been told,
It inspired the Scots into battle in medieval times of old.
The Scots fought the British with courage
And with the spirit of "Hurrah!"
The British won the battles and proclaimed
That bagpipes would be against the law.

The power of music can't be stilled forever, you must know,
And the law became null and void, and then of course
The music of the bagpipes again began to flow!

Though the Scots and the Irish gave the bagpipes
Such great and lasting fame,
Bagpipes were used before the time of Christ
In other lands, I must exclaim.

The image of a man in kilts playing bagpipes, Oh what charm!
He forces air into the blowpipe
And holds the bag right under his arm.
There's another pipe that's called the chanter
Which plays the melody,
Then the drone pipe plays the bass notes to add some harmony.
It sings, it comforts, it cheers us with just a hint of chime,
This is an instrument that has stood the test of time.

All About Paul

(Inspired by a family who lived in Brea Canyon)

Paul's father worked hard in the oilfields
Up in the Brea hills,
Way back in the 1950s,
'Twas a time of active wells and drills.

Yes, Paul's dad woke early each morning,
His pickup climbed that dusty dirt road,
Paul's mother had five small children,
And many groceries she would unload.

"Don't wish for things that you can't have!"
That was the family's robust attitude,
This was their time of hand-me-downs,
And being thankful for leftover food.

Now Paul grew to be an honest man,
Who strived not to be in debt,
He would provide for his wife and kids,
With the physical toil of his own sweat.

There were sunrises, and there were sunsets,
And many seasons passed,
The structure of the old ways,
It seemed to change so fast.

Property taxes, income taxes,
New technology to acquire,
The dollar wasn't worth so much anymore,
Paul thought that he'd never retire.

To send his children to college,
The family budget he would scrutinize,
But college expenses and the cost of living,
Both would quickly rise.

Paul recently had a massive stroke,
From his job he has now resigned,
MediCare and MediCal, they help him out,
And to his home he is now confined.

Society is filled with other folks,
Who are not hard workers like Paul,
They're young, and healthy, and want entitlements,
But never want to work at all.

Our Celebration

We will use our linen napkins
And the white tablecloth bordered with lace,
The crystal goblets and engraved wine glasses,
Our sterling silver in its proper place.

But we're not sure about Uncle Floyd,
He's had a very bad year,
His dear wife, Freda, she died last spring,
For this holiday, will Uncle Floyd be here?

Roy and Marge will bring the biscuits,
And Loretta always brings the relish plate,
And Grandma will say a very long prayer,
While we look at the food and salivate.

But for Uncle Floyd, it's different this year,
He can't sleep, and he has no appetite,
His roof has leaked; his plumbing needs fixing,
And Aunt Freda died on that April night.

Aunt Freda always brought her famous stuffing,
It was everyone's favorite kind,
We'd pile it on our plates and cover it with gravy,
None of that stuffing was ever left behind.

Now, the secret recipe for that stuffing,
Aunt Freda didn't pass it on,
She always served it in that turquoise bowl,
Now, I guess those days are gone.

Oh, Cousin Bernadette—she's changed a bit,
A vegetarian, she decided to be,
She will eat the brussels sprouts and cranberry relish,
Then talk about animal rights and ecology.

Then Cousin Ray would lift his glass
And say, "Let's make a toast!"
We each say something, sometimes in rhyme,
But Uncle Floyd, he'd usually say the most.

But Uncle Floyd, this year he'll probably stay home,
He says he doesn't have a sunny attitude,
Says he doesn't have any jokes to tell,
And can't deal with all that food.

Now, the aroma in the kitchen,
I guess you could say it's like paradise,
The children are laughing and sometimes pointing,
And spirits are quickly starting to rise!

Now the table is ready; let's gather around,
Our yearly ritual we will now begin,
And, then, what's that shuffle sound at the front door?
It's Uncle Floyd—and he's walkin' on in!

Oh, Mister Moon

Oh, Mister Moon, why do you cause some dreams to
come true, but not others?
How do you select which hearts to break?
Do you try to dodge the comets and meteors?
Do you ever reach down to capture a snowflake?
Oh, Mister Moon, why do you cause some dreams to
come true, but not others?
Do you hear the grey wolves howling to you at night?
Do you direct the dances of the whales at sea?
Do you understand the concept of gravity?

Oh, Mister Moon, why do you make some dreams come
true, but not others?
Do you store stardust inside your sleeve?
Do you laugh at man's history books?
Do you remember Adam? How about Eve?

Oh, Mister Moon, why do you cause some dreams to
come true, but not others?
Do you ever hear the songs that are all about you?
Do you glow when no one is looking?
Do you pcck at blissful young lovers during a secret
rendezvous?

Oh, Mister Moon, why do you cause some dreams to
come true, but not others?
Have you listened to all of "Moonlight Sonata?"
Did Beethoven consult you about the harmony and tune?
Do you like "Moonlight in Vermont?"
What about Debussy's gentle "Clair de Lune?"

Oh, Mister Moon, why do you cause some dreams to
come true, but not others?

Traveling On Highway 395

Finally out of the traffic congestion,
So glad to be driving on Highway 395,
Savoring the quiet of the desert road,
It's the peaceful part of the drive.

A few Joshua trees stand in a stupor,
While whispering their secret code,
Creosote bushes embroidered on sand,
Nature's garden near the road.

The little town of Lone Pine,
With Mount Whitney clearly in sight,
And its sporting goods stores and homey cafes,
Not to stop here just wouldn't be right.

Back on the road and feeling renewed,
Discussing philosophy, life, and death,
Adventure in our hearts, freedom in our souls,
And the scent of garlic on someone's breath.

Far from the rattle of urban noise,
Leaving the sound of stress behind,
The landscape spans to the great beyond,
The fountain of youth we'll surely find.

This two-lane road brings nostalgia,
Of long-ago days I reminisce,
When travel was never a generic superhighway,
But a scenic excursion of togetherness.

The town of Bishop lies ahead,
Where the shingles on roofs are layered with frost,
We'll spend time browsing on the charming main street,
Never mind the exact time we've lost.

And now our car is pointed toward the slopes,
There's the fear of falling on my old snow skis,
The journey may be better than the destination,
Like a concerto playing in the pine-scented breeze.

Comanche

These were the people; this was the nation,
Bareback rider on horse, their mighty reputation.
To them, their horses were like diamonds and pearls,
Children learned young, both the boys and the girls.
They rode for training, and they rode for fun,
Comanche and horse seemed to perform as one.
Fighting to protect their culture and their families to
feed,
In battle they could pick up a brother while chasing at full
speed.
No saddles or stirrups, amazing tricks they were taught,
Shooting arrows while galloping fast when they fought.
These were the people; this was the nation,
Bareback rider on horse, their mighty reputation.

Anna de Graf

She was known in the Klondike region as
"Sewing Machine Sourdough"
(Based on a true story during the Alaska Gold Rush)

She was a determined woman, hearty and bold,
Unafraid of the elements, hardship, bitter cold,
Carrying her heavy satchel; seamstress skills she sold,
In a rugged land where hungry men wanted gold.

Like the Good Shepherd who searched for the lost,
She would try to find her son at any cost,
Over crevasses, frozen rivers, mountain passes she crossed,
Boulders, glaciers,—her clothes layered in frost.

Yes, it was her lost son that she hoped she would find,
Trudging through blizzards, her vision almost blind,
Comfort and security she left far behind,
A model of the most courageous womankind.

Arriving at each settlement, she would inquire there,
"Please say you've seen my son!" was her constant prayer,
Rags wrapped around feet were the shoes she would wear,
A testament to the fact that life is not fair.

She survived a long time; strong tents she would sew.
Did she find her beloved son? The answer is *No*.
Self-reliant, hard-working—no one she would owe,
Anna DeGraf. Her nickname? "Sewing Machine Sourdough!"

Chuck Geitner

Teacher—Naperville Central High School,
Naperville, IL—40 Years
Subjects taught—U.S. History, Political
Science
In-Home Tutor, Naperville, IL—10 Years
 Football Coach—10 Years
Athletic Trainer—15 Years
Chairman, Historic Sites Commission, City
of Naperville, IL—15 Years
Coordinator, Veterans Oral History Project
for Library of Congress—12 Years

-Chuck Geitner

The Mystique of the Lady in Red

Why am I awakened as the clock strikes twelve
By an image I cannot delve?
That image, so fascinating, drove me beyond waiting

It led to my creating a picture so captivating
That I could only allow myself a glimpse of the lady in red

The mystique overwhelms!
The brain is fixated!
The image is stamped
Forever on that screen in my head

The lady will always be alive!
How will I survive?
Knowing that I cannot rest, that I shall, forever, be obsessed
By just a glimpse of the lady in red

As I began I end!
The mystique of the lady in red burns in my head!
The lady in red glimpsed in her entirety,
Still a mystique, exuded by...?
Her shoes!

Brown Eyes

Lisa, with those flashing eyes
Makes one realize
What could have been
Had one been keen
On that special day
In the month of May
When men and women
Come out to play

How to erase the years
And then look into the eyes
And hear those phrases
That sometimes lead one into mazes
For this old man
Whose mind can remain
In the domain of his brain

He can float through the marshes
And emerge in the lakes to take the bait that makes
Man appear, from time to time, a fool or a mime
All this is determined by the message that flashes
From those beautiful eyes
Those lovely, brown, flashing eyes
Ah! What a fantasy!

Spring

Philandering
The sun teased the flowering
Roses of the North

My poem, *Storm Watch*, is in the 2013 issue of the *Atlanta Review*.
Two short stories appeared in *The Chicago Tribune* as finalists in the 2011 and 2006 Nelson Algren Awards contests. Other publications include *Imitation Fruit*; *Ginosko*; *Make: A Chicago Literary Magazine*; *Papier Mache Press* anthologies *Grow Old Along With Me*, *At Our Core*, and *Generation to Generation*; *Room of One's Own*, *Faultline*, and others. An evening of my work was performed in the *2006 New Short Fiction Series*, a Live Literary Magazine in Los Angeles.

I currently teach the fiction writing class at OLLI. Before being permanently distracted by grandparenthood, I was a college lecturer in History and American Studies.

I have completed three novels, a novella, and a short story collection. Links to stories published online:
The Tomato Lady
http://www.chicagotribune.com/media/acrobat/2011-06/62275937.pdf
Who Told Me So?
www.imitationfruit.com (Issue #9)
Into the Darkness of Your Absence
http://www.ginoskoliteraryjournal.com/images/ginosko11.pdf
Broken Strings
http://articles.chicagotribune.com/2006-10-29/news/0610290004_1_lucy-shoes-alley/2 -*Rose Hamilton-Gottlieb*

At Laguna Lake

I dance by still water
As the frog in the mud
Swells the rhythm in his throat.

The wings of the firefly
Whisper the melody
As she skims over the pond,
Like stones skipping in sunlight.

My One Red Dress

Red is not my color, but there was a dress,
a shirtwaist, sleeveless, when my arms were young.

Mazatlan red, the color of the open market,
and the color of the warm sea
where we found the abandoned rafts.

The color of the surf we played in, like two children,
I in my red bathing suit.

My one red dress, now long gone,
the color of your white embroidered shirt
that hangs still in the back closet,
the yellowed color of unworn.

Fever Night

A wracking wrecking storm of night coughing,
relentless, unremitting, unforgiving.

Sweat puddles under my eyes,
in hollowed out collar bones,
in that low place between the breasts.
It's raining from inside.

What karma, I ask, brought me to this?

In the medicine chest, half an Ambien,
eight years expired,
pulls me under, then flings me against the wall.

Regress me now to slugship and I'll slither at dawn
over cool grass and gnaw on something green.

Coyote Dreams

After dark they come, the coyotes
with untamed bushy tails and empty bellies.

They cross the highway, all hunger-fed stealth,
to slink around the house, drink from the birdbath,
sniff at the dog run.

They slither through the gate of my imagination
to climb the fence and scratch
at the doggie door of my dreams,
where one chases a small animal into a hole at my feet,
then lopes alongside, eyes yellow and waiting.

Race Memory

I take out the broom to sweep the kitchen,
and Shaineh cringes and slinks away, tail tucked.
"It's not for you," I say.
"Never has been, never will be."

Is it some race memory in her dog brain
of being swept out the door
by an angry housewife in white cap and apron
sweeping the slate floor of her thatched cottage?

Or am I, in another memory, that angry housewife
and Shaineh that other dog?

Watch Dog

She eats the outdoors served up beyond glass,
sliding doors, seven of them, windows to the floor.

From front to back to side yard,
three levels of wonderment.
Here they come, here they are, there they go.
All barkable events.

Up and down and around,
a sunny colored cock-a-poo blur.
Is she celebrating them or protecting me?
I tell her she's annoying me,
but perhaps she thinks I don't know what's good for me.

My neighbor says when I'm not home
she's as quiet as the mouse she would bark at
beyond the glass and otherwise might run from.
Or might not.

Up and down and around,
a sunny colored cock-a-poo blur.
Is she protecting me, or celebrating them?

If I'm not here, are they not there?
It's her world, so I can't know.

I am a native daughter, born in East Los Angeles, blessed with an academic, orator father who read to his children nightly from an early age. In time I did the same for my own 6 children and now I read with grandchildren whenever they are with us for overnight visits. I worked in Title Vll / Title l schools for the majority of my teaching / administrative career in Los Angeles County. It was such a joy to see the lights turn on as children caught on to what reading was all about, first in their native language, Spanish, and then, in English. As a bilingual, cross cultural teacher I was assigned to the newly arrived immigrants with little or no English speaking skill.   *–Alice Gresto*

MLK Holiday Observation

He had a Dream
and I shared it in a
classroom filled with little
black and brown and white children
of the barrio.

We role played Rosa Parks' bus trip
lining up rows of student chairs
in bus aisle formation,
kids vying to be Rosa
or the rude driver.

We sang *We Shall Overcome*
holding hands and swaying
to the music until the teacher
next door complained about
our noise.

Later, in the teacher's lounge
she reminded me
that our loud activities
would not help my students pass
the tests required by

No Child Left Behind.

Arrivederci

Cotton batting clouds cover a patchwork of farms and
villages below.

A glaring white sun illuminates the azure blue
beyond

as we slice through time and space to return to our
own realities.

Ciao, *famiglia*, Ciao, *cugini*, Ciao, *amici*.

Ciao to word game communications

in a scramble of Italian, English, Spanish and mime

stumbling over verbs and vowels with gestures,

raised eyebrows and lots of smiles and laughter.

Ciao to pasta,

round, flat, square, long, twisted, stuffed

anointed in the precious oils, herbs and

pomodori of Umbria, Tuscany and Marche.

Ciao to the heavy roll of cathedral bells

bong, bong, bonging across the piazza,

along the drunken cobblestone alleys,

penetrating the very mortar of ancient buildings.

Ciao to sudden May sky operas

of lightning, crashing thunder and fat rain

met by gypsies in flashes of crimson or cobalt

hawking umbrellas and ponchos made in China.

Ciao to gelato, real gelato,
creamy, smooth, seductive in cone or cup
amarena- cherry, *nucciola*- hazelnut, and
zuppa inglese,- rum, fruit, and cream, oh, yum.

Ciao, to the autostrada
speed lanes, trucks, motorcycles and accidents
laddered road signage designed to take us
to where we did not intend to go.

Ciao to St. Peter's and Vatican Square
jammed with pilgrims, one hundred thousand strong
waving a sea of banners, local and foreign,
chanting, *Francesco! Francesco*!

Ciao, to stairs too far up and too far down,
sculptures, pillars, candle racks, marble, tapestries,
tour guides leading with umbrellas, scarves, beer cans
for a silent glimpse of the darkened Sistine ceiling.

Ciao to verdant Italian country sides
mile after mile of grain, olives, grapes and citrus
farmed over sloping mountains and river valleys
a solitary stone house, red tiled roof, off in the distance.

Ciao, Bella Italia, Ciao

What He Brought Home

Besides the paycheck that kept afloat
a family of eight
Dad was a bearer of gifts
magnificent and mundane.
We all looked forward
to his arrival at the front gate.

During his shipyard days of WWll
there were little tables and
bulky chairs for our dolls
cut from sections of discarded pallets.
Steel remnants, fashioned into tiny hammers
empowered us to pound
brads and rusty nails
into fence posts
for no reason at all.

On days he took the car
into Long Beach,
instead of taking the bus,
we knew we were in for a treat,
deep fried, butterflied shrimp
and french fries from the Pike
just below his office building.

He carried a big canvas bag
on the days he went to the
Long Beach library
to haul back heavy books
of 78 rpm records,
Broadway musicals for Mama
children's songs and books for us.

A glazed tea pot
made in occupied Japan,
a thrift shop discovery,
came in under his rain coat,
another time it was cinnamon rolls.
His lunch pail could be
carrying a new Archie comic book
or an Almond Joy duo
to be carefully cut
into 6 small bites.

Always he brought home
his big Irish smile
and an embrace
that enfolded 3 sons
or 3 daughters at a time.
The biggest hug was reserved
for Mama
who greeted him at the door
wearing fresh lipstick
and a splash of Evening in Paris.

Illegal

A gobbet of grease
congeals in his gnarled beard.
He smacks his lips,
inhales deeply
taking in the sage scented air
in this semi-desert.
Fortunate to snare the rabbit
he cuts it up in chunks
simmers it in the dented
blue and white speckled coffee pot
careful to conserve every last savory drop.

When the glow of tangerine sky
slips below the slumping hills
he will continue his trek north
into the groves of Pauma Valley.
He's heard they will begin picking
citrus near the Indian casino.

His cousin, Jesus, works
in Rigoberto's Taco Shack
cleaning up and cooking
for the big losers
who suddenly can't afford
casino dining.

The sweet dreams of California
have soured for him,
his people are no longer welcome
in these rough times.
A few more dollars from picking this crop
and he will head back to Sonora.
It is easier to starve slowly
south of the border.

Quicksand

tugs at names, faces, dreams,
seeps slowly,
sucks at ideas,
ideals once held so tight
like rules,
rules that could send you
straight to hell.

You lose your grip
you lose your image
startle at the person
staring at you in the mirror
wondering
what became of those saints
that showed you ...
something ...
what was it they showed you

or was it angels
or little children
that appear in your room
saying "Gramma"

but your Gramma...
where did she go,
she was there
in the yard

where is the yard
it was here a minute
ago

and your Joe?

He's waiting
for you...somewhere

A Used One

I wanna used rocker
not a Burlington bright white
nursery rockin' chair
for two weeks pay.

I want an old one, worn and creakin'
with a few teeth marks along bare wood.
I wanna rocker with a broad seat
shined smooth by some granny's wide fanny
eased right out to the support spindles.

I want ancient pecan that carries the hum
of a mother's lullaby, an old farmer's groan
a young soldier's sigh,
upon returnin' from bloody war
that tune of humanity flowin' through the veins
that once carried sap life to spring branches.

I'll rest my elbows along the well carved arms
drop my hands onto forgotten thighs
strokin' old memories with each bend
of my achin' knees.

Rockin' away I'll lend a few refrains
of a long ago love song
that still lingers in my bones.

Wife to college sweetheart Dennis, this year celebrating our 40th, we have two children. Former x-ray technician, recently retired from a city job as an administrative assistant, my retired husband wanted me to join him at OLLI. My Father who had had recently passed away had given me the gift of enjoying poetry, so I started attending Poetry for Pleasure. I look forward to Thursdays, learning of poets, poetry, shared deep thoughts, humor and laughter.

–Jan Hudson

A Moment to Create a Poem

White noise keeps sounds from interrupting sleep
Awake, now, welcoming morning stillness
A distant train whistle—destination unknown
Clock ticking time away, that is never to return
Thought river arises and flows
Pondering attended to
Some thoughts go on list of do
Other thoughts engage in poems
Embracing or purging
Visual feelings, imbedded photos
Get that line on the page
Don't allow thought to slip away lost
Create, elaborate
Simmer, refine
Sit with your words
Read them aloud
Do you hear what you want others to see?

Mor' Papa

Blonde curls surrounding her round little cheeks
She looks up to him as he starts to eat.
A chilled bowl he was enjoying full of ice cream
Behind the kitchen wall, alone so it seemed.
A voice although small was heard to say
"H-m-m mor' Papa mor'," ah, she gave him away.
I asked are you feeding her ice cream before bed
My answer a chuckle and a "mor' Papa" she said.

Dance

Take my hand and step with me
One, one.
Take my hand and walk with me
One two, one two..
Take my hand and dance with me
One two three, one two three...
Just follow my lead, and mirror the melodic tap of my feet,
Feel the flow of the waltz and the Latin tango's beat.
With just one unsure step a dance is begun,
From toddler to child to adult I've become.
I took his hand to step, walk and dance,
My Dad reached out his hand and gave me my chance.

Green 56 Chevy

A large cream colored wheel steered her down the road
Her color was emerald green that glowed
Today was my day to take her out for a spin
Backing her out of the garage was my task
without my passenger jumping out of his skin.
A schooled driver looking back, taking note
Surprised was I when I went forward
and stopped just short of Dad's boat.
With Mom standing at the door looking quite shocked
I was preparing for my error to be mocked.
Suddenly there was a saving laughter
Thankfully contagious shortly thereafter
Another chance I was given
And that's what kept me cautiously driven.

A Great Granddaughter of Immigrants

In 1897 Pasquale Gelardi, passport in hand
From Sicily crossed the Atlantic starting life in a new land
New York greeted him the documents did prove
On his way west he did move
Eventually, a fisherman with his own boat
In the bay of San Francisco his vessel did float
Founder and President of the Crabmen's Protection Union
Seeks the sea before daybreak, after sundown a family
reunion
In August of 1899 Pasquale made Ignazia his bride
She and their ten children gave him much pride
Born, Joseph their fourth child
My Grandfather on which the rest of the Gelardi clan is
compiled
Two sons had they, Pat and Bill
Bill married Joann
And they had Jan

Frederick E. Brye left Germany to escape
When here, going far west for his life to reshape
Auburn in the Sierra Nevada's is where he settled
Being town mayor and butcher is where his energy was
channeled
Annie and Frederick had five children, the last being twins
In 1900 the life of Chester and Lester begins
Grandfather Lester married Juanita in 1923
One daughter had they, Joann
Joann married Bill
And Jan is their oldest girl

From a line of two immigrants I am created
As my parents complied family history has so well stated.

Navy Grandpa

Together they sat Grandfather and Grandson
Reading and testing until they were done.
Navy literature was being reviewed
An American sailor was about to make a debut.
High school graduation first had to take place
Before the journey began to his training base.
The same day OJ's bronco sped through the towns
Daryl put on his cap and gown.
Soon after we heard pomp and circumstance
He was transported to Chicago with expedience.
Boot camp letters describing adventures
From June through September were received with
pleasure.
Correspondence was not just with family
There was the garbage collector Hector and Luigi.
And then came the marching of the sea of white
To Anchors Away, oh what a sight!
One sailor amongst others on the blacktop he stood
In the bleachers his family; importance of ceremony
understood.
Then the tour of Chicago, going where we shouldn't have
gone.
And managing to turn the Sears Tower parking alarm on.
Ending our visit with an Italian restaurant dinner
Grandma and Grandpa guarding Daryl's uniform to
make sure there was no red wine splatter.
Flying back home, as proud as can be
Was now an American Sailor's family.

Christmas Will Be Different

Crystalizing moisture blankets landscapes
While inside steaming mugs, and a warming hearth
lend to an escape.
Churches and neighbors lovingly assembling nativity scenes
For our heart must remember what the season means.
The shoppers fill the malls buying their special gifts
Hoping to cross off all the names on their shopping lists.
A cookie-stained recipe waiting to come to life
Chocolate and vanilla scents lessen our strife.
Warm greetings and good wishes, addressed to family
and friends
Stuffed, stamped and ready to send.
Parties to attend, meals to prepare
Oh, don't forget that special outfit to wear.
Christmas time is here, just like last year
But this year is different and won't pass without a tear.
Traveling miles won't bring us together
But memories of Christmas' past will last forever.
Merry Christmas, Dad.

A Presence from Nature

A kindred spirit to something larger
Petite lines reaching for the light
Colors displayed in the seasons of life
Showing there is beauty in strife
Verdant oasis springing forward
A scent of freshness gently floating into the air
Welcoming shade as the canopy grows
The sultry heat in the wind that blows
Splashing hues of red, yellow, orange
Pausing to reflect in the warmth
Nature's kaleidoscope of brilliance
An artist's pallet of fallen colors
For some their work is done
Dry and brittle they no longer hang on
Fall—ending the journey that they had begun.

Sharing Pain
(Colorado Movie Theater Shooting 7-12-12)

Balloons floating toward the heavens
Grievers left below watch as the separation grows
Candles flicker with an air filled with sadness
Flowers adorn the grounds of those walking with a heavy
heart
From a distance our nation watches as their emotions
seep into our being
An unexpected sharing
For some empathy for others sympathy
Each step a little slower
Heads down a little lower
Some of us have been taken again
By one of us, what happens then?

Dashes and Numbers
(During 2012 Olympics)

You start with a number
Your starting point to be a member
You begin in a safe serene place
You're set in the blocks ready to run the race
You start your journey through the canal
Your track is the map for you to become a final
You roar as you clear those newly formed lungs
You're hoping the training was enough
            for what needs to be done
You receive blankets in which you are swaddled
Your heart, legs and arms pumping at full throttle
You feel her warmth, and the softness of her voice
Your finish line is in sight, so now make a choice
You are the hope of those that brought you into this world
You're the hope of a nation watching trans world
You aspire to make your entire life worthwhile
Your dash is your whole life for you to compile
You end with a number
Your ending point to have been a member

A Gift of Time
Post Retirement

"In the desert of the heart
Let the healing fountain start."
Auden

And then one day there was time to...

Write a few verses in the serene darkness of the morning
Go back to sleep and awaken without an alarm warning

The soothing warmth of coffee for the second cup
While snuggling with a furry friend pup

Striding on a path draped in nature
My heart pumping life that needs nurture

The warmth of the sun seeps through my skin
Surroundings to which I am emotionally kin

Pages to envelop to enhance my thoughts
Writing the poetry that unties the knots

Creatively preparing a meal for nourishment
Ah... some red wine for an unwinding refreshment

Perhaps some theatrical entertainment allowing an
escape
Resulting in stimulating conversation that helps reshape

The sun now has long since hidden itself
Sleep comes easier when taking care of myself.

Essence of a Distilled Poem
From a Rookie on an Edit Committee

Lines moving across the screen
Readers' interpretations heard
Processing grammatical perfections
Writer rejects or accepts

Syntax, ellipsis, spaces, quotes
Writers yearning to express
Narrative verses

Childhood memories, family homes, vacations
Observing parental gestures
Contributing essence to adult character

Spouses expounding their compassion
Recalling marital moments
Forever, years later to their beloved

Blanketing pages with memories
Adult travels, special occasions
Purchased or inherited memorabilia

Thoughts coming through a labor of love
Birthed and refined
Writer of a perfected poem

Born in Canada. Lived in Vancouver, B.C. until the age of 22 then married and came to L.A. Writing poetry was never in his thoughts until Betty Tang suggested he come to a poetry group at OLLI in Fall, 2012. That started the ball rolling. He has now written about 90 poems and enjoys hearing from the eclectic group at Poetry for Pleasure. They never cease to amaze him with their talent.
          –Allan Koven

Remedial Living

I was 10, a wannabe cowboy;
but then I grew up

I was 17, a Socialist I thought
but then I grew up.

When I was 22, marriage called hard upon me,
but I grew up.

When I was 30, Life gave me a son
quickly I grew up.

When I was 36, divorce, marriage;
and with cool composure, I grew up.

What should I say about that sad day at 63
That I grew up? Hardly.

Here I am ...married again.
Still showing up, still growing up.

Life has taught me that
Nothing remains ...at an age
It's learning to become
What God wants from us
And it's all remedial.

Sixth Sense Seduction

In ordinary ways
in ordinary days
I stand before her quite amazed
at her lithe form.

While reaching up to touch a cloud
with naked limbs (it's all allowed).
Her beauty strikes though not to lure;
to transform me of that I'm sure.

I hear the whispered wind blow through...
to once again say its adieu
...in delicate sound, so very crisp
upon this newly blossomed tryst
like falling leaves that gently touch
a waiting heart.

While still in trance of blessed bliss
I knew that a presumptive kiss
would end this convocation.
And so in silly awkward glee
and truly thinking it was not me
I could not I resist; oh won't you see?
It was not wrong to hug that tree

Beauty Abides

Beauty abides, and as her lover,
I lift her veil to see transparent eyes glimmering
with an enticement worthy of seduction.

Touching some primordial passion,
she wreaks havoc on my senses.
And graces me with unspoken words
that promise delightful pleasure.

Beauty reigns as Queen supreme.
Upon her throne she emanates majesty
with an exquisite demeanor and
I stand back intimidated and shy.
Who can reframe this emotion?
Not a poet or artist's brush.

Her soft rolling hills and gentle valleys;
expectations of undiscovered treasures
fire an imaginative pose.
I am bound up in a mystic rush
that dominates like a drug's addiction.

An in an exotic haze I lie dreaming
of ephemeral caresses,
highly charged currents
that flow unrestricted around
her coveted reactive spaces.

Alone, with thoughts in time displaced,
I wonder, does she entrance all others?
Or in my silent muse am I the only one
transformed and felled by her abstract beauty?

Her allure is enduring, enshrined for all to see.
The recherché picture of her memory
never grows old and she still remains
indelibly imprinted on my erotic mind.
A beautiful woman or a mountain valley?

Day One in a Poetry Group
(hyperbole and surprise)

Walking from the parking lot I was flooded
with fearful alarming thoughts that seemed to fuse
into a catechism of what I knew was about to occur.

Poetry? How could I enter the dungeon of your secrets?
I imagined being shackled and hanged in pedantic chains
and whipped into linguistic shape by a grammarian.

Would I be able to withstand the overwhelming torture
of critical examination? It felt like a masochistic
virus had been let loose inside.

Quickly glancing around the room
it suddenly appeared to me
that I looked like a caught prey in a lion's grip
being taken to its pride.
A vague mental paralysis began to grab hold
so as I quickly took a place meant just for me
sandwiched between two obviously vacant chairs.

My voice crackled in a dissonant high note
as it stammered out an unctuous introduction
to another inmate.
The ax had fallen.
(pause)

My first day in the poetry group, you ask?
Really; It wasn't so bad.

Heat By Degrees   (a semi erotic poem)

Feathered shivering fingertips
give way to erotic heat by degrees,
the hot-cool beat of lovers in cadence.

If, when on this journey of perplexing events
one learns about love's secret itinerary,
it would be wise to remember,
passion invites, the possession of which
varies in heat by degrees.
With most individuals, save a few,
like a drug it subdues withdrawal pains
for just a short time.

84

When the caresses have begun to mellow,
trysts, in heat by degrees, again start to ascend
stealthily lurking, to buoyant rising from
places deep in the corrugated shadows
of man's frenetic mind.

Infused, and fired with singular intention,
heat by degrees unabashedly exposes
greater levels of agitation and rushes forth
unrestrained by any rational reasoning.

Ah, but when basted by the tested
and proven love of blended familiar flavors,
the savoring of remembered exotic delights
becomes richer and more pleasing, and
the heat by degrees flames evenly
and ever so slightly down, waiting for love
to be served at just the right temperature.

An Anthropomorphic Muse... From Where I Stand

I stand tall, erect in the morning light
and sing my silent praises to you.

The night wind blows in a sacred dance
and sings its praises to you.

The earth below me holds me in a firmament
and reveals its praises for you.

My bow bends as enchanted echoes
resound in praises to you.

As my skin sheds and falls
I rejoice in praises for you.

For you are life,
the beginning and the end
the source and flow
of all that exists.

And for all these miracles
praises don't suffice;
but just the same from all our kind,
forests large and orchards small,
samplings new, and trunks quite tall,
we thank You in praise everlasting.

Talking To Me

Do you ever get the feeling that inanimate objects are
talking to you?
Sometimes I do, not often, but sometimes.

Like trees that seem to be murmuring in an unknown
language somehow suggesting a meaning to me.

And clouds when billowed tell me of some distant place I
haven't visited.
They display portly faces that look strangely familiar and
seem to mouth broken words.

Once I heard running water in a stream ripple in nomadic
sounds, it told me the secrets of how to go with the flow.

Flowers often, when in full bloom, gossip and say "look at
me, aren't I beautiful?"
But when dying cry out say "I was younger then, but now
I'm old and frail!"

It seems when picking out socks to wear, I imagine them
vying for my attention.
"Pick me... no pick me," and when I do, feel a little guilty
that I didn't pick the other.

Once I took out and put back pliers from my tool holder
on the wall. One cried out to me saying that I shouldn't
put it so close to the other one (considered far inferior).
And of course, the screwdrivers made it known that
Phillips do not belong with Flatheads.

86

Should it be, do I have to endure these insults to my
sensibilities?
As I said, sometimes.

Waves

If one compares the ocean's wave
to life upon the human stage,
minds conjure salt water sea
and know forever's meant to be
in blowing winds and moon pulled tides
bridges to the world's divides.

These metaphors are thoughts aligned
that pay no heed to warning signs
that say life's many noxious ploys
are games to play, as water buoys.
Ships that move along the ocean's core
all here today and gone once more
dashed upon some distant shore.

Absorbed in unconscious realms sustained
by clouds encased with thunderous rain
that bluster forth its moisture spent
upon the water's firmament.

And where will all our history go
to poet's rhyme and thoughts that show
we are more than just a wave?
Our lives are played and soon engraved
in song and verse albeit saved
in memory's graceful reverie.
unlike the ripples of the sea.

The Old Pier (a picture poem)

beneath the boundary layer of air and sea
twirling vortexes of frenzied waters
incessantly corrode
the aging pillars below.

the ravaged tired timbers emit
anguished unholy screeching sounds
as ocean swirls beat nonstop in and about
worn out planks attached beneath
the weathered decking.

the riddled concrete sideling emerges
perplexed and whistles out its
protestations in echoes heard
across the raging tide.

in the bottoms underflow snail infested
warped planks buffer incursions of countless
schools of rabid predators that attack,
conquer, and devour unsuspecting aquatic prey.

above fishermen pray to the sea gods
to hook their water worn lines and capture
in songs of surrender the call of
a waiting bucket.

in timed release, ancient messages splash upon
silicon sharpened shores that resonate the sounds
of strident hungry seagulls
rummaging for their next meal.

wave upon wave of scattered foam wash over
brash crayoned streaks of blue and green hues
that seem to melt across and blend into
a continuous pallet of assorted colors.

at the same time the formidable forces
of untamed waters compete
in their final rush to win
the race to land's end.

A POCKET FULL OF MIRACLES
Once upon a time there was this crazy fun-
loving woman who wasn't sure what she wanted to do
with the next chapter of her life. Time marches
on so quickly. Her kids are grown; they have their own kids, and now
the grandchildren are old enough to be off on adventures with their
lives.

Now, what adventure was she going to experience? She likes to sing,
act and share her spiritual beliefs. She likes people, animals and spur-
of-the-moment happenings. It's good to plan things, but often, if plans
don't pan out...oh well...she is in good health and financially okay.

Her life has started a new chapter of freedom. Sometimes she gets
bored and that gets her motivated to try new things. She doesn't get
over busy, nice and easy is her motto. She reminds herself of all the
things in life for which she is grateful. A life full of drama is now in
balance. The other day someone told her kids, "You better keep her on
a leash." Stay tuned for the next episode.

Reverend Doctor Marcella Matthews
a.k.a. Marci

License Plate Frames
Messages from Angels

My father's name was David Byron Matthews. Everybody called him Barney. He was a wonderful person: father, grandfather, and friend. He worked in construction, and one of his favorite things to do was to go to the horse races and win that money! He had a great sense of humor and a positive attitude. He was always ready to help anyone repair anything. He was not only my father but also my earth angel, always helping our family, enjoying life with wit and laughter.

When he was 90 his time on earth came to an end. His spirit left his body on 11-1-2007. I went for a long walk that day thinking about our life together. I saw a license frame that said, "Daddy's Little Girl." What a blessing to see that message from him that day.

His birthday was February 6th and on that day a year after he passed, I went to a restaurant we used to go to. I drove out of the parking lot and the car in front of me had a license frame that said, "I'd Rather Be at the Races." I said, "Hi, Dad, good to hear from you."

Watch those license plate frames for a message "4 U 2."

Kevin McGrath was born in Pasadena, California. His love of poetry and words manifested itself during his time in high school.

His influences include: Ray Bradbury, Shakespeare, Dickens, Edgar Allan Poe, e.e. cummings, Bob Dylan, Dylan Thomas, Leonard Cohen, The Beatles, Jack Kerouac, Allen Ginsberg, William Carlos Williams, Robert Lowell, Pablo Neruda, Walt Whitman, James Joyce, Jimmy Buffett, Jimi Hendrix, Ernest Hemingway, John Steinbeck, Monty Python's Flying Circus, Woody Allen, S. J. Perelman, George S. Kaufman and Moss Hart, Neil Simon, Paul Simon, Bill W, Bill Hicks, Richard Pryor, Lenny Bruce, George Carlin, Charles "Sparky" Schulz, John Coltrane, Miles Davis, Joni Mitchell, Bruce Springsteen, Stephen King, Steven Spielberg, Walt Disney, George Lucas, Martin Scorsese, John Wayne, Clint Eastwood, Marlon Brando, Tennessee Williams, Jack Nicholson, Jonathan Winters, Robin Williams, David Crosby, Bing Crosby, Bob Hope, Johnny Carson, Bill Cosby, Laurence Olivier, Stanley Kubrick, Franco Zeffirelli, The Grateful Dead, Captain Kangaroo, Howdy Doody, Bozo the Clown...

He currently lives in Orange County, California with his girlfriend and two cats.

–Kevin McGrath

I Wish I Were In Love Again (For TH)

Frank Sinatra laments & I sympathize.

Time takes its toll.

What was once new, exotic & erotic

is now familiar.

We have our own routines-

our regular routes—

shorthand—

We've forgotten to really look

See, Feel, Experience, Be

in the moment.

We sometimes feel the pull of egg timers, schedules,

appointments

& we forget to take a breath,

until this morning.

I slept in until the sun warmed my face through the

bedroom window.

I was dragging myself into consciousness

when she walked in with the eight week-old kitten.

Rory is a calico like her mother & covered with brown &

black splotches over her white coat.

Her green eyes widened at her new surroundings.

We were waking up together eyes blinking, hands &

paws scratching, limbs stretching.

Terry walked in with coffee, handed me a cup & laughed

at the kitten & me,

looking bewildered on the bed in the cloudy sunlight.

I absorb

her laugh

      her thoughtfulness

her smile

      her tenderness.

Then I remembered.

It all came back.

This is a new day.

A gift.

And I realize

I am in love again.

Your Own Personal Song

Let go of the idea that you need to be an expert.

You're a folksinger, you're with folks,

just show up and sing.

This is story time.

Just imagine a campfire on a fall evening.

Our faces are lit in the glow of the yellow and orange

flames.

We're relaxed and happy.

We're safe.

There is no TV or radio.

You have to make your own music, sing your own song,

tell your own stories—

So, take your turn.

If a note cracks in your throat, that's real, that's the story.

No one lingers on mistakes as long as you keep going.

Stephen Stills once remarked that he'd made a career out

of singing out of tune,

off key, or something—I wasn't there, how do I know?

The point is that nobody cares as much as you.

If you can let go of care, of self-consciousness, then

you've got something.

Those cracked notes, those sliding pitches, those uneven

rhythms are your own personal song.

It calls us home.

It sails us across seas.

It propels us into nature

and introduces us to ourselves.

There are no overdubs in real life so sing out.

Hit whatever notes you can.

It's all just part of the music.

Walking the Fence

I remember looking at the moon, all alone at the back

door of my childhood home.

In the world of my backyard memory the avocado trees,

the swing set, the metal slide—

are all seen in black and white.

The moon and its craters appear closer than in real life.

During the summer I used to balance myself and walk

along the rail that topped the six foot high redwood fence

that bordered the property on my side of our house.

I wish I could still trust myself not to fall

like I did as a young daredevil when I walked that fence.

Perhaps I deserved the punishment.

I'm sure that I was guilty of the offense but when my

father slapped my face

I was so shocked that surprise surpassed the physical

pain.

I landed hard and sprawled across the grass.

The body landed several feet from where my father's

powerful forearm propelled me.

I never managed to get back inside the body.

I remember getting home after my father took me to

deliver newspapers on my route one afternoon.

From the moment I jumped from the truck I was running.

I wore a fresh haircut.

The wind rushed cool past my ears as I rounded the

house,

ran into the backyard and threw myself on the ground,

and I rolled and rolled and rolled through the freshly cut

grass.

I can smell it now.

I wish that I could trust myself not to fall, and to roll in

the grass again

and not feel foolish or wrong.

I wish that I could have all that silly-sad-foolish fun

all over again, and give up the trappings of stoic

adulthood.

Sometimes I feel like I never stopped running in my high top tennis shoes

with the sun still hot on my neck and the smog biting at my lungs.

Running from contact.

Running toward the moon and the cool lonely night.

Running from the barking dogs and the smell of dinners.

In my mind I still walk that thin beam trying to balance myself

hoping to prevent the fall.

Nothing prevents the end of summer and the return to school.

I follow the path to where the nuns wait to line us up and march us into class

in time to the martial music.

After all these years

I'm still running, still marching—

still trying to balance myself between the sun and moon

and the world of fences.

I'm still looking over my shoulder

dreading the slap and the fall

and the smell of grass suddenly in my face.

Still I keep throwing my feet at the ground

attempting to break the fall.

The memories of summer

keep me playing in the backyard dirt.

There I remain amid the crashing leaves,

the potatoes, and rabbits awaiting slaughter to feed our

large family.

Still I keep trying to break the fall.

Today is another sunset

another moon

and I'm still in the backyard trying to walk the fence.

godi (for e. e. cummings)

godi think of myself sometimes as

godi do sometimes imagine myself as godi do i

sometimes do

& i think godi think

         does this mean I'm crazy (?)

no i say to myself no thati know that godi know

that godi do know some things & goddamni know that

sometimes

i goddamn know thati sometimes know

         what i am doing (!)

      but not this time

godi wish the helli knew this time

'cause godi know

thati don't know this time

Vacation Beach Mexico

The clouds continue

writing their current address

across the blue late afternoon sky

A glowing sun

does its familiar job

it doesn't stop for orphans

or the wind

Freeway trucks

travel south (this being holiday)

Accordion jovial in the distance

Land Rover creeps

5 dark birds glide unflapping

on the final crest of sunshine

skeleton clouds of fish

prehistoric animal white

paralyzed in the fading afternoon

bright

to the last second

I live with my husband Rolf in Whittier. My two married sons live close enough for me to babysit my 3 precious granddaughters, 4 year old twins Maddie and Zoe and 16 month old Colette. I've always enjoyed poetry, and created my own song lyrics to sing along with my guitar since age 16. As a fourth grade teacher, I always found a way to incorporate poetry into my classroom, and I'm guilty of exposing my students to "haiku fever." I really enjoy sharing poetry now with my OLLI friends who I admire and respect as poets and treasure as dear friends. *–Jan Mendez*

This first group are seasonal Haiku about Yosemite:

Spring

Sky falling water
 wind feathers you to a veil
  Merced draws you home

Snowmelt swells the streams
 that babble down the mountain
  springtime serenade

Pine shadows on snow
 a collage in gray and white
  early spring palette

Summer

Moonlit cloud sailors
 gliding through the midnight sky
  gauze-sails all aglow

Face turned toward your face
 I bask in your borrowed light
  moonlight in forest

When I'm in the mountains
 my heart feels like it's home
  essence of be-ing

Fall

Swiftly moving clouds
  you're gathering together
    for the big snow-show

Golden oak leaves float
  gently to the ground in a
    somber dance of death

Dressed in burning rust
  you make a splendid showing
    before dropping robes

Winter

Spiny carpet of
  frozen needles in ice
    texture the pathway

Ice diamonds sparkle
  shimmering in the morning
    capture winter light

Clumps of white pile up
  in soft sculpture on the ground
    frosting undisturbed

Earth Day '07

Don't miss the small glorious moments
   The way words bumping against each other
Turn into a beautiful simile in a child's poem
   The way a small bud on the tree
Turns into a flamboyant dogwood blossom
   For a short time in a Yosemite spring
Don't miss the universe of a dandelion seed
   Blown to an awaiting world

Sometimes, waiting for the big-time, earthshaking
experience
  We miss the small mysteries and miracles
We miss the magic in a smile or a seed
  Or a beautiful harmony

*****

Lord, help me see the small
   bright miracles around me
     magical moments

               A seed holds promise
                  massive oak in the future
                  new hope embryo

Look at little things
  raindrops grow to be a river
    flowing to the ocean

Emily—A Poem to Emily Dickinson

Emily—like a nun in a cloister
  You viewed the world
From an upstairs window

Like a caged bird longing to fly free
  You dreamed of love
And ecstasy

You never flew far from that upstairs window
  But the view of the world you gave us
Was infused with reality and sensitivity
  You made us see the world we're in
With clearer, more perceptive eyes
  Although you only viewed it from afar

How ironic that you on the periphery
  Could give us such insight into
What we ourselves are blind to

Like Vincent showing us the beauty of a starry night
  From behind his veil of madness
You gave us a vision of a world
  You experienced from a distance

Maybe the one apart can better see
  The way things are
But how sad to have felt so deeply,
  Thought so perceptively,
 Seen the beauty in the smallest of things
And never really to have left that room

You touch me and warm me with your glow
    Even though we are separated by worlds of time and
place
That is the power of words and wisdom
    And the glory of someone who sees beyond the
ordinary
And can share that vision
    Someone who can give us wings to fly
Although earthbound
    Someone who can look at the ordinary
And see the sublime

Dragon Flight

For my granddaughters Maddie & Zoe

Maddie and Zoe went walking one day
    To see what they could see
They got up to the top of the hill
    Where the wind blew wild and free

Under the rainbow waterfall
    Was a dragon that they spied
They crept close and softly asked,
"Please, sir, we'd like a ride"

He lifted them gently with his tail
    And slid them on his back
With a whoosh of wings and fiery breath
    And a sound like a thunder crack

He caught the wind and soared so high
    They thought they'd touch the sun
With loop-de-loops he swooped and dove
    They never had such fun

And when the sun was setting
    And stars glittered the darkening sky
He took them back to the mountain top
    And let out a dragon sigh

"I have to bid you two goodnight
    And send you on your way.
But you both know what you'll dream tonight
  —a dragon flight all day."

They gave the dragon a goodbye kiss
    And followed the path back home
And dreamed of flights on dragon's wings
    And adventures as they roamed

Having completed both undergraduate and graduate work at California State University, Fullerton, she received her B.A. and M.A. in Fine Arts, Design and Photography.

Her career focused in the fields of ideation, branding, marketing, merchandising, packaging and display design. She created for such firms as Microsoft, Epson, Canon USA, Neutrogena, Crayola, Calaway Golf, Geoffrey Beane, Sunkist, as well as many California wineries. She built and worked with outstanding design teams and received both national and international recognition, many awards and acclaim for exceptional design throughout her career, including two CLIOs.

Interspersed with this creative work has been a contribution to the educational field, having taught fine arts at California State University, Fullerton as well as Riverside City College, Mount San Antonio College and Laguna College of Art and Design.

The mother of one adult son, she currently travels, continues to design and paint, reads everything and writes often, especially personal poetry, does crossword puzzles daily, great cook, appreciates good wine, loves to garden, collects fine art and antiques.

–Veronica Michalowski

Whispered

Lying nude, they spoon
Softly
    Slowly
        Words emerge
Sincere, trusting
Committed, whispered phrases—
Louder than any shout
More potent than a consent
The heart and soul of a vow.

Body Landscape

Sunny Arizona morn
Cool breezes, pale sapphire sky
I begin to sketch the branch and detail of drying
      Sycamore leaves
      with Autumn grass below
My pencil stops on the grainy alabaster surface—
      my mind wanders to what it dreams to
      interpret . . .

    Wise baby blues
    Dimpled cheeks
    Smiling mouth with upturned edges
        restless to begin a kissing foray—
        deep and timeless, tongue
        exploring each cell it can taste.
    Neck curve meeting the strong, wide
        shoulder
    Curvaceous deep shadow where bicep
        touches chest wall
    And the hands—those gifted arm tips
        with contrail fingers—
        anxious to stroke and dance anew
        on womanly mounds and folds.
    Solid pecs, textured nipples
    Rippling abdomen
    Triangular form of the hips
    And the maleness that swells intensely
        when aroused and brings the
        shrill of ecstasy when thrust
        and exploded.
    Gentle curve of the back and rounded
        buttocks
    Powerful, muscular thighs
    Angled knee, shapely calf
    And feet that walked a thousand miles.

This nude is what my eyes hunger to see—details until
     known,
     memorized from every position;
To feel again your body landscape and hear its
     rhythmic heartbeat.

How long?
How
    long
       is
         the
           wait?
When will the feast begin?

Gardens

Where is the garden that gave us life,
    filling our sights with varied
    hues and beauty?
It was there not so long ago.
Hidden, the seeds and spores await
    a new beginning to nourish
    the souls of others.

* * *

Gardens
    are the visible
        expressions of the forces
        and cycles of life and death.

* * *

Each soul embodies a
blooming garden within.

Mystique

We were ready at our easels for class to begin.
She's a new model; we'd never sketched her.

She disrobed and began with ten-second positions.
> catch the action
> rhythm of the body
> work fast and loose
> don't think
> just draw
> respond to what you see and feel
> no detail
> broad strokes

move the charcoal <u>across</u> the paper.

She sat; face crouched in bent knees, fingers touching her
toes
> moved her arms above her head
> knelt with waving hands
> brought her arms down and stood,
> began walking slowly in a circle
> > capture the form
> > don't stop
> > respond to the movement
> > grab the charcoal
> > illustrate the posture's repetition
> > don't linger in one spot
> > shift the figure
> > sketch, sketch again
> > quickly
> > faster
> > use the whole sheet
> > another sheet

Interpret the pose.

Next, she lay on the mat, propped by pillows;
    A ten minute sketch.
    Move the easel
    get a better position
        more time for detail
        use softer charcoal
        accentuate the shadows—
           make them pitch black
        get reflections from the skylight
        emphasize the mid-tones
        be seduced by the figure
        describe the softness
        use the side of the charcoal
        smudge with the finger
        fashion a background
    Interpret the pose.

Finally, a thirty minute sitting.
    Relax through the drawing
    Use brush and ink
        fill the paper
        look hard
        scrutinize
        embrace the image
        portray it all
        emphasize the curves
        make the setting exotic
        include the texture
        more detail of the pattern
        configure her as beautiful as she is
    Interpret this nude.

Class is over—she's finished.
She dons the robe and leaves the studio.

She's not said a word and with this muted silence
Created a mystique, an aura and gave it all to us.
No artist could ask for more.

The Boxer

He came in smiling and offered a hug.
No handshake here, he was physical from the start.
We ordered lunch, wine and spoke of our lives.
52 winning bouts,
Traveled the world
For his military branch.
54 matches and 52 wins,
Doing as young man what he did as a boy
In the neighborhood.
He learned why it was important to win
To never give in, to give it his all.

Grandfather was the local Don
And only grandmother could reach him
But always later, always in private.
As the oldest, he understood his familial place,
Being a leader was thrust upon him;
He grabbed the role and created his own reputation.
He loved the power and local glory
And carried it into adulthood
Knowing he would follow the path
Of his Mother's father.

54 matches and 52 wins,
He rested his laurels on that success.
But the war and the ring injured and changed him,
He could no longer physically fight.
Grandpa died. Someone else was in charge
And he was free.
To do what?
How to succeed after
54 matches and 52 wins?

He worked decades to arrive
At this small café and openly
Tell his story
Without fear, without shame.

110

He had failed and stumbled
And finally accepted
That his best would always be
54 matches and 52 wins.

He loved women, he said, but did not
Understand his two wives.
Commitment, trust, devotion
Would be different now,
Had to be. He took a risk
Coming today, to start anew,
To win in this arena.

We joked and laughed
And he asked about my life.
The summary was enough
To make him enthused again.
He wanted to prevail with
54 women and 52 wins.

But women are not opponents, I said
We're in your corner.
There's no winning here,
Just loving, dependent upon
Each other. Forever.

He'd never had that,
She was always a foe;
True intimacy would be new
And he asked for patience.

Learning that skill takes time—
Did he have enough?
Where would he get the strength?

I like you, he said. Could we begin now?
I'll call you tomorrow.

And never did.

Freedom

He flies . . . he soars.
He's twenty-something again.
Methodical, disciplined
Structured and strong.
He asks for weather reports often.
He's safe and treasurers this gift
Of climbing with eagles,
Into the sun, living in heaven
With illusionary clouds by day,
Planets and stars by night
Above the green, azure
And lights of Earth
If only for a while.

His respite, his release,
His calm.
It's where he is his truest self—
Real to the core,
Unpretentious,
Confident.
He understands the delicacy,
The risks,
Adventure
Of ascending into air
Viewing infinity
And topography
In one frame.

He treasures this freedom
And will do all he can to keep it—
Stay healthy, fit, sharp, not give in.
Beyond the family he created,
He loves this environment most.
A pilot—he leads.
He soars.
He flies.

My parents read to us. Those peaceful evenings formed memories not to be forgotten: "Wind in the Willows," Robert Frost, my father's favorite Canadian poets, and beloved others. How precious those evenings remain. "Rabbit Hill," the story of Beowulf, King Arthur, and much more formed our love of literature for both my brother and  me. Those smoky evenings by our coffee-colored velvet couch left words as memories. Our family treasures were leather-bound books and paintings from our father's travels. At Potomac School in Washington, DC, high school in my hometown of Falls Church, Virginia, and the College of William and Mary, I loved to read and write. Moving to California, divorcing young, I raised three young children alone until marrying my husband, Marion. I earned both BS and MS degrees at UC Irvine and spent my career with defense electronics systems, mostly at Hughes Aircraft Company—but always reading and writing for myself and family.   *–Jane Anderson Moon*

Virginia Springtime

Early chill morning: tiny crocuses
Peek through softly melting snow
Holding hints of spring to come
While forsythia buds bulge
   Beneath our bare maple trees
   Waiting for Springtime to come.

Across the road small houses sit
Silent in morning's yellow light,
As dawn blends dusky rose to
Greet new day and welcome
   Our family on our way, off past
   The woods for another busy day.

Hidden in woods, little foxes play
While wood-mice scurry through leaves
Among ferns water droplets fall
Beneath the trees, where small creatures
   May drink their fill, then
   Search for tiny morsels.

As days pass, green spears appear,
Narcissus open to fragrant white, and
Daffodils burst in yellow clouds
To greet each fresh new day. Then
   Vivid pink crabapples and flowsy
   Peonies burst in joyous welcome.

In our house rich fragrances: peony,
Bridal wreath, such gorgeous loveliness
In pewter jugs and crystal vases
Bring springtime into evening
   While we listen to Chopin and read
   'Wind in the Willows' with delight.

Down the road the horses are getting
Frisky, dancing in their corrals, eager
To trot dark paths in woods and along
Open roads, celebrating spring is here.
   Our time for galloping across the fields
   Has finally come—such joy!

We children play in the old garage,
Climbing high in dusty lofts filled with
Forgotten treasures from decades past:
Old brass bedsteads, satin quilts, frilly
   Petticoats and cotton dresses,
   Grandma's embroidered pillowcases.

 Hours we spend gazing into misty
Mirrors, arranging chairs and tables as
Our dining room from the 1930s,
Fancy tablecloths and glass dishes,
   Spring flowers as a centerpiece
   Plucked from Mother's garden.

Now the house stands silent, vacant, no laughter,
No news broadcast on the radio.
Children's happy games only memories,
My attic bedroom bare but well
    Remembered—the music, laughter, and
    Grandma's things treasured in my heart.

New Hampshire Summer Day

Sunshine high and hot among the fields and trees,
We amble on roadside, picking Queen Anne's Lace
And kicking pebbles from two hundred years
Of farming here along this trodden path.
    Over there a deer peeks from among the trees.

Hidden in woods the blueberries grow
Ripe and succulent, just right for picking.
Into our pails they go, along with Black-Eyed
Susans and tiny treasures found along the way.
    Best of all, we love wild flowers.

Down the road in Uncle LJ's barn the kittens play
Where our friends are swinging high above old
Lofts full of treasures from decades past, those
Ancient trunks filled with white Victorian
    Petticoats and frilly cotton dresses.

We spend hours climbing ladders and
Peering into wooden boxes,
Wearing stiff corsets and high-topped shoes,
Arranging bedsteads and dressers just
    As they would have been a century ago,
    While Diggy strokes the kittens.

In the garden, warm yellow tomatoes are
The sweetest we have ever known,
Delicious juices running down our chins,
Icy cold lemonade in flower-painted
  Tall glasses celebrating summertime!

We watch the field so green, where the cows
Are munching, moving gracefully through
Tall grasses, sometimes mooing gently
In apparent satisfaction. Yes,
  Even they love warm summer days.

In evening, Uncle LJ herds his cows
Back into the lower level of the barn,
Safely in their places, where they will
Settle in for a calm, uneventful
  Night to rest until morning sunrise.

How memories of the summertimes of
Childhood, so innocent and loved, still
Remain vivid—the beloved grandchildren
Of my parents' friends now turned old and gray,
  Their own summers shadowed and forgotten.

Autumn, My Memories

How we watched the clouds drift by,
Lying beneath the apple tree,
Looking through its gnarly branches,
Dreaming of autumn showers
  And chrysanthemum bouquets.

Foxes trod through the woods nearby
And owls sat in trees, surveying
Vibrant reds and purples just across
The silent road that twisted
  Between gray rock walls.

The old red barn in silence slept
Beneath amber skies, all cloaked
In faded gray from passing time
And sleeping years, dogs dozing
    In sunny patches, dreaming.

Some days, we walked under crimson
Tree branches near our stream,
Watching sticks and leaves drift by,
Floating down to hidden places
    Where squirrels buried secrets.

In autumn, deer browsing in golden
Fields moved languidly in the sun,
Contented to be warm in afternoon,
Looking forward to evening's silent
    Bliss, warmth, and rest.

Ah, how we picked grasses along
Country roads and in among the fields
And trees colored orange, red,
Brown, watching sleek foxes
    Trotting toward their den.

In evening-time, you lay sleeping
On your cot, lolling away the
Time for mellow celebration,
Smiling at secret memories.
    My treasured friend.

Watching for Winter

How I dream of birds all puffed up,
Feathers full to protect from winter's
Chill winds, brilliant cardinals on snow,
Chickadees, blue jays, and winter's owls
    Busy with their preparation.

Silently, I watched the clouds drift by
While bare gray branches—still—at twilight
Shivered in bursts of wind, while houses
In our village nestled calm and warm,
    Holding families safe, content.

From under the rooftop gables
We watched the night descending,
Its black curtains hiding everything.
Only our big pine tree in silence
    Anticipating snow season.

Yes, how we mused in evening's
Lonely splendor, waiting, watching
Snow soundlessly drift onto sidewalks
And windowsills, all seen
    Through wavy glass windows.

Deep in dusky woods, owls snuggled
Among dark tree branches, watching
For a storm, but only the gentle snow
Fell silently, while small animals
    Settled in comfort, safely hidden.

Yea, tucked into secret places
Among roots and leaves of winter's
Season, they still huddle: foxes,
Bears, chipmunks, and field mice
    Safely, warmly napping.

Ancient Worlds

Lo, five thousand years past time remembered,
Cruel world of peasants, warriors, and slaves,
Most humble yet strong, used for building.
Hauling. Pulling. Working under sun in
Unremitting, endless days of pain,
These men building empires in rock and sand.

Now the Great Wall stands strongly connected.

Who were these ancients? Why their slavery?
What their achievements? To whom renowned?
All for glory, empire, eternity.
Who were the emperors, and why such zeal?
For their glory and fame eternal.
Behold the powerful. Submit to HIM.

Ancient roads lead to majesty and awe.

Four thousand miles from China to desert
Sands blazing under sun, desiccated,
Men rushed to nothing, meaningless,
Men wasted for an eternal vision
Hidden in wind and crumbling rock,
Not breached in a thousand years of trying.

Yea, we struggle toward eternal life.

Camels ply the Silk Road in search of treasure,
Shifting endlessly under brilliant blue,
Plodding endlessly under burning sun.
Is it worth the life of a camel?
Should a man die, crushed under the sky,
All for empires, rock and sand, for glory?

The leaders die. Only mystery remains.

Santa Margherita Afternoon

Only yesterday, strolling pathways beside
The sea, seagulls wheeling in mad spirals
Sweeping overhead high above the palm trees,
Mysterious walled and scented Italian gardens,
  We passed ancient mossy houses.

On pebbled paths, old stone alleyways,
Carved doorways and shuttered windows
Hid grandmothers, families, and their
Activities of this May afternoon. Were they
  Napping, dreaming of long-past summers?

Indeed, peaceful walled gardens with masses of
Vivid bougainvillea, tinkling fountains, and
Frothy fruit trees seemed to beckon us.
But we dare not turn that handle to enter
  These private spaces or peek inside.

High on rocky cliffs far above, we gazed at
Tiny boats bobbing on gentle waves, yachts
Moored in the crescent harbor, and far-away
Ships traveling to distant places; we paused
  To savor the sleepy town and lazy beach.

Back down beside the sea, we found a tiny café,
Bright umbrellas, empty tables, and busy
Waiters setting up for afternoon guests,
The chef selecting tasty morsels, his
  Stove with hot coals at the ready.

Ah, our memory of languid Santa Margherita
On a weekday afternoon, rocky cliffs and
Sun-kissed places, elegant houses delighting us!
Today, sitting in Café Lucca near our home,
  Warm memories bring peace and joy.

I was born in Los Angeles, California, and except for my service in the Army I have lived most of my life in southern California. All of my college education, including a Masters Degree and a Teaching Credential, was accomplished while I worked full time to provide for my growing family. In the end I was pleased with the academic degrees and credentials I achieved and my lifestyle improved accordingly.

But, following all of that the earning of a Black Belt in Kempo Karate entailing seven years of continuous training was my most personally satisfying accomplishment. It was a long and arduous endeavor. When I retired from my careers in business and education I joined OLLI and have enjoyed the pursuit of favorite hobbies and activities. Some of these were new to me and others I simply didn't have the time for in the past.

My first and foremost goal in life was to have my own large loving family. I believe I have been blessed with that. I have a beautiful wife, and my family grew to include 5 children, 11 grandchildren, and 3 great-grandchildren. At this moment the family continues to grow and thrive.

-Patrick Oswald

20th Anniversary - June 6, 2011

Twenty years ago Brenda and I
stood upon a southwest facing beach
on the Hawaiian island of Kauai,
and were married in a beautiful private ceremony.
The sun glinted off our rings
as the minister held them up—
a beautiful rainbow filled the sky.
Then another gentle rain misted the air
and strangers standing by applauded our joy.

It was a good day and a favorite memory.

Halloween of my Youth

In my youth Halloween was mostly for kids—it was all
about costumes
      made from whatever stuff we had at hand.

Recurring favorite characters for my younger brother
and me were pirates wearing bandanas made from our
little brother's
      laundered diapers (plentiful and never missed).

Cutoff jeans were always sought for days before the
event—by end of summer ours were nearly spent—
   hems were freely loosened, cut and torn—
      by Mom (of course)

Left over wooden stakes from the picket fence Dad had
made were used to create sturdy swords—
   old shirts modified by removing collars and sleeves
      provided really good tops and vests, we thought.

Lipstick and mascara applied strategically—once again
   by Mom—gave us a final touch.

But the best costume I ever wore was that of a headless
horse-less man while I sat on a kitchen chair
   monitoring candy treats from our covered porch
      just by the front door.

Mother made the outfit from an old butcher's white
cassock – that had belonged to her long deceased father.
Wire coat hangers were formed to lift the shirt above
my shoulders—garden gloves were attached for
      hands—a red scarf shoved in the neck supplied a
     bloody stump.

I sat nearly motionless near the pot of candy and
jangled a heavy chain when visitors approached to help
themselves to the treats.

But when I stood up moaning eerily even adults ran
quickly away screaming.

Spring Emerging Again

Following a long cold winter, spring was emerging
—bursting out everywhere.

Butterflies had unfolded from protecting chrysalises.
—the yard was aflutter ... in a myriad of vibrant
and iridescent colors.

Erupting blossoms beckoned hovering hungry
hummingbirds to plunge their rapier bills into floral
throats full of ripening nectar.

 A clouded cluster of heavy bumble bees
arose from a purple-blue bush as I approached.

A scattering of lizards (some tail less) scurried across
paving stones and up the block wall ...
to escape ... household cats.

Boisterous birds filled the trees—chittering and
chattering, they attacked the seed feeders
hung out for them.

Then as I passed by—returning to my kitchen
the whole multitude fell back with a swoosh into
        a line of tall sentinel evergreen pines
        and were almost silent—

But I thought I heard a whisper from the trees—
"Be aware, there goes the Giant—
        he might come back again!"

Haiku Summer Musings

Early morning breaks
Orange-vanilla candles smoke
Hot shower wakens

Just by my window
Yellow rose buds opening
Scented winds blow in

Hot days brilliant skies
Endlessly oppressive heat
Cats doze - lizards hide

Scattered clouds drifting
Warming winds barely blowing
Crushed ice - cooling drinks

Sun sets heat withdraws
Sidewalks cool flag falls listless
Night things fly about

Blazing hot morning
Suffocating afternoon
Smoking hot mowers

Kick back Saturday
Baseball - football all day long
Heat wave keeping on.

Oh What A Beautiful Autumn Morning

 I slept late that morning waking to a beautiful autumn day, with a cool crispness in the air and the sun shining brightly without burning. A feeling of restfulness surrounded me while arising from my bed with only fleeting thoughts that I might continue sleeping.

Then while taking pleasure in a leisurely shower and listening to a favorite weekend radio show with songs emanating from the 30's and the 40's thoughts of Dad swept through my head.

Remembering him listening to the same sounds in days gone by, now this enchanting music is what I too enjoy. Perhaps the music was, and is, comforting because it's what I grew up listening to, maybe even before I was born, until "Rhythm and Blues" began to insert itself with a different beat and urgency.

That morning felt especially soothing and I found myself singing along with the old familiar songs - then I heard an instrumental of "Oh What a Beautiful Morning"—it seemed so right on that autumn morning.

Cranberry Relish and Other Stuff

Cranberry relish, hot apple cider, butternut squash and
pumpkin pie with plenty of fresh whipped cream—
roasted turkey, mashed potatoes with gravy on top—
and plenty of stuffing—just the delicious kind.

Linen napkins with embroidered maple leaves
of gold, red, brown and sienna—

Family gathered 'round the table—
brothers, sisters, uncles, aunts
and cousins—and all of the children of course.
A prayer of thanksgiving and joy is offered
by everyone there—

Outside the air is filled with crispness of autumn—
leaves falling—our spirits rising—
We make a toast to each other and all that is good.

In the Pursuit of Peace

In the passionate pursuit of peace,
our vulnerably flawed and wounded nation
aggressively avenges unprovoked assaults,
to oppose outrageous and oppressive subjugation
by those who continuously assail and ensnare
unprotected and blameless people everywhere.

A Special Yellow Rose

An oil painting of a yellow rose hangs in my study—
a new blossom unfolding as heavenly tears trace across
petals drooping while a single twinkling rain drop
    rests upon an uplifting segment.

This treasure, a long ago gift from my eldest daughter
 now sadly passed away, was received by her from an
aspiring teenage beau—but his family wouldn't let their
budding
    romance grow.

Knowing of my then artistic avocation and believing
my appreciation for her friend's skillful talent,
she trusted that I would give his endeavor lasting care
    and affection.

Since then the golden rose remains in that special place
reminding me of its delicate grace while just by the
window a yellow rose bush grows allowing me to see
    new flowers as they come to be—

As I enjoy their fragrance, in the springtime,
 lightly drifting through the open window
    seemingly just for me.

Cicero the Advocate – *A Narrative Poem*

On a hot Roman Spring morning
in the year 80 BC,
the young advocate, Cicero,
confirmed his oratorical skills
to defend a wealthy citizen,
Sextus Rosicus Chrysognos.
He had been accused by the emperor
Lucius Cornelius Sulla and others
of patricide and would soon
be formally convicted and would surely die.
However, Cicero's oratory overwhelmed
the Senate and even tyrant Sulla.

Sextus was summarily acquitted
and a celebration ensued
whereat in a drunken stupor
he admitted his quilt.
Alas, then he was brutally murdered
by a disapproving wealthy matron
with a thrust of her long steel hair pin
into the base of his craven brain.

Subsequently, Cicero was asked
if he was disturbed that the man
he had defended was guilty after all.
Not at all said he—there is no dishonor
in defending a guilty client,
but there is honor
in embarrassing an outrageous tyrant.

So, after all the centuries
nothing has changed
for those who profess advocacy—
it's only a game that they strive to win,
if only for the sake of winning.

Ronald is originally from Louisiana and arrived in California after joining the United States Navy in 1967. Upon discharge from the military in 1971, Ronald settled in Long Beach, California. He attended and graduated from California State University Long Beach and San Diego with degrees in psychology, social work and public administration. His professional career included work in government as a licensed clinical social worker and fiscal administrator, university lecturer in public policy and organizational management and a private practitioner of psychotherapy. His interests include physical fitness, golf, philosophy, theology, ethics, poetry and African and African America histories. Ronald views poetry as a means of liberating the self.

-Ronald Pierre

Mademoiselle

She moves about guided by unspoken appetites
Nurtured in her heart by hopeful expectations
of intimate encounters while immersed in blasphemous
fantasies

She negotiates the vicissitudes of daily life, work, family
and social relationships with a swagger of left, right
rhythmic motions
Motions that are sometimes staccato and other times
legato

She makes no proprietary claims on anything external to
her heart
She demands no respite and pays no homage to the
unceasing syncopations of her biological metronome

She lives, she maneuvers, she cast about and conquers,
after which, she retreats to the solitude of her heart

Oh, Mademoiselle.

The Mystery of Love

We stood together in a familiar place in the summer cottage where we swore our love to one another. We were near the wooden stairs with a large window to our left, through which we gazed and imagined our future. The evening air was cool like the time our hearts first came together.

She spoke first and recounted for me the many times we promised to love one another. I listened, though silently wishing she would not go on, but I knew she had to. With the moon as our witness, we revisited each emotionally murky tract of my infidelities and failed promises, as well as her sleepless nights shrouded by migraines of guilt and sadness.

I tried to conceal my hurt by consuming glasses of Southern Comfort, but to no avail. She continued to dagger my heart and senses with allegation upon allegation. I attempted to look away, only to be confronted with my guilt reflected from the vase we once cherished.

I wanted so much to reach out and hold her and to tell her how sorry I was for causing so much pain and disillusionment, but I could not bring myself to do so.

She moved closer to me. I immediately felt the urge to escape, but as I stepped back, the wall that had been listening denied retreat. I continued to silently petition a higher power to intervene.

Forced to look into her eyes that were reddened from the weight of tears, I spoke. "Are we really here?" I was overwhelmed, because standing before me was the one woman that I ever really wanted and loved. My head began to swirl while I felt her warmth, gentleness and sincerity of heart. With an arrhythmic heart and the night growing late, I shouted to her, "Can you love me again? I need you to love me again. I never stopped loving you." She did not immediately respond.

With the ensuing silence weighing heavily upon me, I searched for refuge by staring at the floor, while I feared my ears would rupture from the pounding of my heart.

Unexpectedly, she passed her fingers through her hair as she approached me. Leaning toward me, she smiled and whispered, "As the moon is our witness, I believe we shall love again."

In a state of complete exhaustion, dilated pupils and moist palms, I extended my arms and surrendered all of me to her. She received and embraced me, then we closed the shutters, turned off the lights and slowly began our ascent up the stairs, with warmth and hope of a new beginning in our hearts.

Sisters Syncopating

Sisters Syncopating

Their hearts are filled with longing for one or the other to
say an inviting word.
Each desires to join the other and find a means of
permanently deconstructing the barrier that inhibits
them from uniting their hearts.

One sister is older but both are burdened with common
hurts and disappointments, unacknowledged birthdays,
Christmases without a tree or gifts and parents not
present at school events. But still with their voices they
attempted to penetrate their internal barrier of conflict:
a sense of hopelessness and a belief in possibilities.

Sisters Syncopating

The pitch of their voices rose while they tearfully recalled
a time spent together, one sister prepared their mama's
hair, while the other set makeup to her face. "So much
fun," the younger sister whispered followed by silence
and gentle swaying and groaning.

Sisters Syncopating

Separated by insecurities, bonded in blood
Each sister silently petitioned her God, grant me another
dawn of day, wherein my heart may find my sister's
heart.

My wise and wonderful parents taught me that one of the highest achievements of mankind is artistic creation.

So whether I am creating characters' lives on stage; exercising creative problem solving at work; capturing a glimpse of a model's soul in a portrait painting; transforming notes on a page into magical sounds on the piano; or arranging thoughts, sounds, and rhythm into a poem, I continue my search for that elusive goal.

- Elizabeth Daron Redmon

Poetry of Autumn

(Upon the occasion of a class assignment to write a poem about Autumn)

Ah Autumn!
Was there ere a poet who hath not writ his praise to thee?
Alas, probably only me.

Oh Autumn!
Do you not tire of the participial phrase?
Blushing trees, whispering branches, waning days?
Can you still delight in descriptive leaves?
Pirouetting, rustling, or just falling from the trees.
How many allegories can you tolerate?
Lost love, later years, a pallet of paint.

Ah Autumn!
Though I love the joys you bring to my home
I just can't bring myself to write you yet another poem.

The Blue Danube Waltz

White sail billows free; bright sun...red heat.
I race to the wind; blown hair...bare feet.
The freedom I feel...on the swell...
Makes me young, and vast, and well.   All is well.

133

Priorities

At seven I was on my way to a gold Olympian medal.
You see, I had long legs and was a good jumper.
But it's hard to find time to train
When you have to practice the piano.

But that worked out well.

At 13 I could hear the applause at Carnegie Hall.
You see, I played with great drama and flare.
But my fingers made lots of mistakes
So I wisely transferred my talents to the stage.

But that worked out well.

By 17 I was sure to be a Broadway star.
You see, I imaged myself a second Carol Burnett.
But suddenly rehearsals became a drag—
A boy asked me for a date.

But that worked out well.

I would be named World's-Sexiest-Wife and Mother-of-
the-Year.
You see, I liked to think I was a domestic femme fatale.
But it's hard to ooze sex appeal
While chasing toddlers and wiping poop.

But that worked out well.

I awaited the Pulitzer Prize for children's fiction.
You see, I wasn't going to let rejection letters hold me
down.
But you can't raise two sons alone without income,
So I took up writing about cancer research.

But that worked out well.

My team would win the Nobel Prize for Medicine.
You see, I worked for leaders in the field.
But electronic technology opened new doors
So I helped develop a medical website.

But that worked out well.

Millions awaited me, just like Bill Gates or Steve Jobs.
You see, the technology bubble hadn't yet burst.
But the effort was underfunded
So I returned to a new role in university administration.

But that worked out well.

I would prepare to wear a College President's hood.
You see, I knew how to climb the academic ladder.
But retirement age approached
And I craved time for travel and art.

But that worked out well.

I'll be hailed as the new Picasso or Rembrandt.
You see, I've toured and painted five continents.
But I can't paint today --
I'm babysitting the grandkids.

But that works out well.

I am the perfect grandmother.
You see,
> I can jump on the trampoline with Samuel,
> Play the piano and write stories with Sarah,
> Dress up for play pretend with Grace,
> Help Matt with his college application,
> And paint pictures of them all.

And that works out very well.

Oops, gotta go.
I have a doctor's appointment at 2:00.

Two Boxes of Gratitude

With loving fingers I lay the quilt
Into my first gratitude box—
My life in bits and pieces,
Carefully chosen selections
Pieced together with scraps.
With gratitude for the fabric that has become my life
I top the box with a beautiful bow.

With loving fingers I bring before me
My second gratitude box.
Thankfully I leave it empty—
The accident averted,
The soldier returned unharmed.
With gratitude for the stresses of fabric that didn't tear,
I top the box with a beautiful bow.

Feel Your Way Gently

Feel your way gently into that dark place
Where inner sorrows stalk.

Pierce that void cautiously
As shadows attack.

Breathe the air slowly
Before oxygen fails.

Scream your loss quietly
Because agony echoes.

Then cry uncontrollably
For tears can heal.

"I thought I would like to illustrate your poem, but I think
I really wanted to have a poetic conversation. Your poem
touched a chord that is common to every individual--and
probably most vertebrate animals as well. I was
reminded of a quote by Lui Chi, '...I am alone with beating
of my heart....' Here is my poetic response to you."
Rayleen Williams

Deep Recesses

In deep recesses where I sleep
Shadows haunt and fears creep.
These are places I do not wish to visit,
As dark silhouettes just wait and sit.

Slowly, cautiously, I crack the door
Until light floods that basement floor;
Exposed, the shadows disappear,
Dissolving all the fathom fear.

Hidden deep within my being
My shortcomings I feared revealing,
But once I faced them in the mirror,
Deception was no longer the allure.

Passing storm clouds now bring
Renewal, dissolving mistakes' cruel sting,
Drenching soil, land, and earth
With disinfecting tears for my rebirth.

— Rayleen Williams

Ole Amos

I met Ole Amos in a small Georgia town—
The most intriguing man I ever found.
I started to talk as we sat around,
But Ole Amos—he just spoke with his eyes.

I asked Ole Amos about his life—
Have you been single or had a wife?
Have your years been filled with peace or strife?
But Ole Amos—he just spoke with his eyes.

Did your father work in the diamond mines?
Or the vineyards making, or drinking, the finest of wines?
Did he give to you wisdom, his love, or his time?
But Ole Amos—he just spoke with his eyes.

Did you sit with the youth at the five and dime?
If you went to jail did you pay the fine?
Did you follow those laws of no reason or rhyme?
But Ole Amos—he just spoke with his eyes.

So I stopped talking and quietly sat still
Though I knew he must have stories to tell.
We silently shared thoughts of Heaven or Hell.
Ole Amos and I—we just spoke with our eyes.

I have been both an OLLI member and a Poetry Class member since 2005. Both have enriched my life immeasurably—the people who gather together to celebrate each other's love of poetry, creativity and curiosity.   – *Mary Sampson*

"The cure for boredom is curiosity; there is no cure for curiosity."—Dorothy Parker

September 20

The party was already under way
When he arrived.
He had his eye patch on,
A fake hook on his hand,
Scruffy hair partly covered by a bandana
And a four-day growth of beard.
He even had a stuffed parrot on his shoulder.

He rang the bell
And when the door opened,
He bounded into the room shouting,
"Avast, ye landlubbers,
Get me a tankard of grog
Before I make you walk the plank,
Ye scurvy knaves!"

All eyes were upon him.
Slowly, it dawned on him.
"Isn't this a pirate party?
Isn't this Talk Like a Pirate Day?"

"No, that was yesterday."

The One

Snow swirling around the mountain
Darkening the day
Men and women in assorted uniforms and protective
armor
Roam the wooded slopes and search the cabins,
Slogging through the deepening drifts,
Searching for the one who drew them all there,
The one who destroyed lives,
The one who left false trails,
The one who eluded capture.

We watched the news as the son we loved
Crouched in the snow with his fellow officers,
Shielded by trees,
Waiting for the one sought, to attempt to flee.

The one who finally surrendered
Himself to his own deadly weapon.

Landscape, with Goats

Chain link fence partially draped with
Shreds of wind-blown, green plastic sheeting,
Stands between a busy street and what is possibly
The last piece of open land in town.
"Open" is a misnomer.
There are two, maybe three, houses
Semi-obscured by untrimmed trees and bushes.
The buildings, in various stages of disrepair,
Sit amid the clutter and debris of lives that have
Become more than they could cope with.

The fields between the widely scattered houses
Are inhabited by every imaginable abandoned object:
Travel trailers
Pick-up trucks
Refrigerators
Five gallon paint buckets
File cabinets
Trash barrels
Cars and fragments of cars
Lawn mowers
Machine parts of indeterminate origin or use--
All nestled comfortably in abundant weeds
All covered with a fine patina of rust.

I've never seen anyone come or go from any of the
houses,
But there is life in those fields.
About twenty-five or thirty goats
Call this home.
Ambling among the detritus of their environment
Keeping the weeds in check,
Munching thoughtfully.
On hot days they gravitate toward
The meager patches of shade from
The scraggly trees that struggle
To survive in the arid fields.
They hunker down there
Until the shadows steal away.
One by one, the goats get to their feet
And enter the new shade location,
Cropping a few more weeds en route.

An emu also lives in the field.

Poem Noir

A lamppost glowing yellow
In the steady drizzling rain in the night.
A trench-coated figure
Emerges from the dank, fetid alleyway.
He leans on the damp bricks
Of a boarded-up bodega
And lights a cigarette.
The flash of the match
Briefly illuminates his face,
Revealing a mouth
Made cruel by an angry red scar.
He waits.
He waits.
The cigarette glows orange,
Grows shorter.
He checks his shoulder holster.
The drizzle continues.

He waits some more.
"Click   click   click"
Faster
"Click-click-click-click"
Until it stops.
He drops the butt of the spent cigarette,
Twists his shoe to rub it out
And moves forward into the
Wet yellow pool of light.

"Hey, baby, you're late.
I thought you might not come."

The sinuous figure whose
Click, click, click of her red stiletto heels
Had announced her approach,
Responds breathily,
"You big lug, you know I'm drawn to you

Like a moth to a flame.
You're bad for me, but I can't help it.
You make me feel so good."
He pulls her lithe body to him
And presses his lips
To her voluptuous scarlet ones.
They remain locked in the embrace
As the drizzle becomes a steady rain.
Finally, they part,
And with his arm firmly
Around her shoulder,
They walk out of the
Dim amber lamplight and into the noir

Two Hares on Campus

I followed the walkway
In no particular hurry
Then stopped,
Arrested by slight movements
On the grass.

Two brown, furry things
That I realized were rabbits,
Their ears erect and alert,
Their tales truly resembling
Cotton balls
Or some other cliché for white and fluffy.

I stood transfixed
As one hopped into the shrubbery
In no particular hurry.

I waited for his companion
To join him in their shelter.
I was reluctant to move on,
(Even though I had somewhere to be).
Preferring to remain
And watch this vignette of
Lapin Life.

Social Network

Fire Hydrants
Street light standards
Bushes
Tree trunks
Telephone poles
Even bus benches—
All dogs stop,
Sniff,
Sniff again, Make their marks,
Sniff some more,
Circling,
Sniffing to see who has been there before
And what messages have been left.

Pee mail

Sniff, mutt
Sniff, mutt
Sniff, Lab
Sniff, mutt again
Sniff, Ooh! Big one! Mastiff
Sniff, mutt
They all checked in at the Canine Social Network.

Not Face Book--
Tail Book

Overstuffed

His lime green corpulence
Inches slowly across the tomato vines,
Munching as he goes
The buffet of verdant leaves.

Mr. Hornworm is not yet sated.
Onward to the prime edible—
The large, green globe at the end of the vine.
As he chews thoughtfully,
He notices that it matches his own skin.
How serendipitous!

Finally full, his head nods;
At least, it seems to be his head.
It looks the same as his hind end.

When Mr. Hornworm moves forward on his
Barely perceptible, stubby, little legs,
It's definite which end is the head.

He drops to the dirt below and goes on his way

Until...

A large, dirt-encrusted work boot
Rises up, hovers,
Then stomps on Mr. Hornworm's rear end.
From Mr. Hornworm's front end
Spew his liquidey, limey green contents
Across the garden and onto the other tomato plants
A warning to Mr. Hornworm's hungry relatives.

The Darker Dark

I lie in the dark of my bedroom,
Dark once I turn off the light.
I arrange the covers just so,
Folding the top sheet over the quilt.
I am careful not to let a careless foot
Or hand hang over the side of the bed.
I know that there is a witch
That lives under my bed at night
And she will grab whatever limbs
That overhang the bed and drag the unwary child
To the Underbed Netherworld.
What happens there is too horrible to contemplate.

Limbs safely tucked in, I still can't sleep.
The closet door is still open---
The darker dark that is in the closet
Is more frightening than
What's under the bed.

Gathering my six-year-old courage,
I leap from the bed,
Slam the closet door
And dive back into the bed,
Almost in one movement.
I snuggle down,
Safe at last from the darks of
Under the bed and inside the closet.

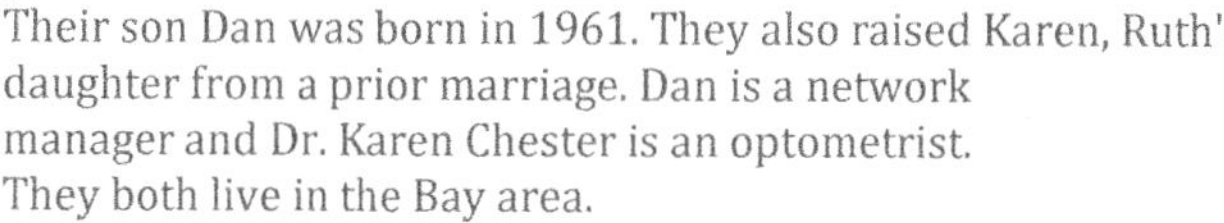

Ruth is the daughter of immigrants from Eastern Europe. She attended the City College of New York (now CUNY} and received a B.S. in Education in 1952. She then moved to California and attended UCLA, earning an M.A. in English. She taught English in junior high for a few years.
In 1960 Ruth married Ted Shapin, a computer pioneer who worked at Beckman Instruments. Their son Dan was born in 1961. They also raised Karen, Ruth's daughter from a prior marriage. Dan is a network manager and Dr. Karen Chester is an optometrist. They both live in the Bay area.

During the Vietnam War Ruth operated a Peace Center in Santa Ana. She also worked as a draft counselor at Cal State Fullerton. In 1979 Ruth entered Western State College of Law in Fullerton, graduating in 1983. She passed the Bar and joined with Donald Buchanan to open a law office in Santa Ana, specializing in Social Security law.
Ruth and Ted joined OLLI many years ago while it was still known as CLE, and began attending the poetry class. Many of Ruth's poems reflect her deep-seated commitment to peace and social justice. In 1988 she and Ted joined with Jews, Palestinians and others to found the Cousins Club of Orange County which works for peace in the Holy Land. *-Ruth Shapin*

One Human Family

We are all one human family,
A rainbow of races,
Ethnicities and faiths.
I dream of the day
When all the nations
On this earth
Shall sit down together
And covenant
To destroy all weapons of war
And live forever in peace.

On that day
The children of this world
Shall rejoice
For their future will be secure.
On that day
The billions for war
Will be used to end poverty
And provide a free education
For future generations.
On that day
Hatreds will melt away
And we shall embrace
As brothers and sisters
And work together
To sustain our planet Earth.

Reflections of a Senior Citizen

I used to think
That I would reach
A resting place some day
Where I would simply be
A passenger on planet Earth,
Drifting with the universe.

But now I know that life's
A never ending race.
We rise each day
To meet the test,
Another plea for aid,
A sudden burst of rain,
A leaky roof, a swarm of ants
Parading on the kitchen floor,
An ending or a new beginning.
A friend dies, a child is born,
We mourn or fill with joy.

Life speeds on,
A comet streaking by,
Until at close of day
Our spirits mingle
With the stars.

Sanctuary

At 5 a.m. the men from ICE*
Knocked on Maria's door.
Fearfully, she let them in.
Her kids, a boy and girl,
Came running to her side.
"Mama, mama," they cried,
"Why are they taking you away?"
She could not tell them
How many years ago
She crossed into the USA.
Maria pleaded for more time,
Just one more day.
To her relief, they said, "Okay."

Maria gathered up her things,
Grabbed her kids, and hurried
To a nearby church, a House of God.
The good folks saw her plight
And gave her sanctuary.
There she stays in fear,
Hoping that the men of ICE
Would not dare
To take her from a holy place.
She prays that she can take her kids
Back to their home some day.

*U.S. Immigration and Customs Enforcement   (ICE)

The Death of Oscar Grant

A Black mother weeps
For her dead son.
"I'm in God's hands," she says,
"He will heal my heart."
Still I want to know why
Her son had to die.
Why did the white officer
Shoot a young Black father
Lying face down
On a cold Bart platform
In the early dark hours
Of New Years Day, 2009?

No answer comes to mind,
Only a deep sense
Of something gone awry,
A long history of Black men
Dead before their time - Emmett Till,
Medgar Evers, Martin Luther King,
James Chaney and his white friends,
Andrew Goodman and Michael Schwerner,
Civil rights workers,
Murdered in Mississippi,
And nameless others
Hanging from trees.

History moves on. A Black man
Sits in the White House.
We are told to celebrate
The end of hate in America.
Yet Trayvon Martin recently
Was murdered by a vigilante.
And still I wonder
How many more Black mothers
will weep? How many more
will lose their sons
To an early grave?

When will we eradicate
The demon of racism
That still haunts America?

Email Blues

What did I do before email?
Read a magazine, read a book.
Went for a walk around the block.
Now I'm a slave to email.

Sometimes I hear the refrain,
"Didn't you see my email?"
"No," I confess,
"I played hooky that day.
I went to the gym,
Attended a meeting,
Met with a friend
Face to face."

At night, though I'm tired,
I usually check my email.
And what do I see?
My mail box is full!
Dutifully, I delete, delete, delete.

Yesterday I told a friend.
"I'll send you an email."
"I don't do email," she said.
What? A rebel? A free spirit?
A Luddite? A dinosaur?
Is she missing out on messages
From the world out there?
She doesn't care.
She has time to spare.
I envy her.
She's not a slave to email.

Note: This poem was writ by hand.

Foreclosure

(Based on a story in the newspaper)

She stands outside her home,
A sheriff is at the door
With an eviction notice.
Her home is hers no more.

A small child stands at her side,
A scared look on his face.
Will he have to leave his friends?
Will Mom find another place?

Foreclosures flood the market,
This is America's shame.
Thousands suddenly homeless,
Wondering who's to blame.

The system is broken,
Folks are in despair.
But the story isn't over,
Change is in the air!

A new day is dawning,
The people will have their say.
No one should be homeless
In the USA.

Competition

Athletes at the Olympics
Compete for the gold.
Workers compete for jobs
To stay out of the cold.

Bankers take houses
From the poor every day.
People die of illness
Because they cannot pay.

Nations compete for resources,
For oil and much more.
This deadly competition
Eventually leads to war.

Can we build a different system
In our land of the free?
One of cooperation,
Peace and harmony?

Can we all learn to share
The wealth that we hold?
Can we care for the poor
Instead of the gold?

Can we have full employment
In our economy,
So folks can contribute
And live with dignity?

Can we give an education
To all of our young
So they can learn skills
And feel they belong?

We can have food and shelter
And Medicare too,
Basic rights for all,
For me and for you.

A Beautiful Day

It's a beautiful day
in Orange County, USA.
The cottony clouds
Are scattered across the sky
And sunshine brightens the way
As we drive along
Surveying the sun-lit trees
And the hills beyond.

It's hard to believe
That somewhere in Waziristan
A village in Pakistan
A mother mourns the death
Of a beloved child, as she
Wanders through the wreckage
Of her war-torn home.

Night falls in Orange County.
We drive out again
To enjoy a dinner and dance.
The night time sky
Presides over bright buildings
And cozy homes.
In Waziristan the rubble is lit
Only by the distant stars.

We live in a cocoon,
Sheltered from the drones
That kill and maim
And yet the cries
Of countless victims
Haunt our days
As we go about our lives
Here in Orange County, USA.

Ted Shapin was born the day before Armistice Day in 1927. He received a Bachelor of Science degree in Electrical Engineering from the Illinois Institute of Technology and a Masters Degree from the University of Illinois, where he helped build the Illiac, one of the first electronic computers. After retiring from Beckman Instruments, he joined the Continuing Learning Experience program (OLLI) at Cal State Fullerton where he helped set up a computer lab to teach oldsters how to use the Internet.
He is married to Ruth. They have a daughter Karen, a son Dan, and two grandsons that they enjoy visiting.

–Ted Shapin

Doors

We have a lot of doors in our Eichler house besides the front door.
Three glass doors open to our backyard garden,
two glass doors open to our atrium with its plants,
one wooden side door to the bushes outside our house.

It is not uncommon to find a cricket walking around inside.
If it's a young cricket, I can catch it in my hand
and throw it back outside.
But yesterday I saw an older one walking around.
When I approached to put my hand near it,
it took a powerful jump backwards and scurried away.

Later when it came crawling by,
I took a small rug and dropped it on top
which stunned it before it could jump.
Then I picked it up and threw it into the atrium.
That was my good deed for the morning.

Oranges

When we bought our second house, it had been built on land
from an orange grove.
One orange tree was still growing on the front lawn.
Unfortunately, we didn't know how to take care of it.
Eventually, it stopped growing.

We make orange juice before our breakfast every day.
We have a motorized squeezer made long ago.
It makes juicing easy.
Summer time is the height of Valencia oranges.
This morning one large orange filled an 8 ounce glass.
The juice was delicious.

At year end, Valencias will stop and Navels will begin.
Navels are mainly good for eating, not for juice.
I did find one grower who comes up from Mission Viejo to the
local farmer's market with Valencias,
when local growers have none.
Eventually, in the "colder" months, we usually buy frozen
juice from Trader Joe's

Silverware

When I was a child, we had a dining room in our second floor
apartment.
Two windows looked out on the back yard of grass.
My father had his garden along one fence.
Women hung their wash on ropes between poles in the yard.

Mother had an expandable walnut round table in the center
of the dining room.
She had a walnut china closet
with a curved glass front door for dishes
and a walnut table with drawers for silverware.

We had real sterling silver cutlery. It was pretty when it was
polished, but got tarnished easily.
Mother had to take out cloths and polish it.
When Ruth and I got married, we received silverware gifts
from my eight aunts. I didn't want to keep it.

I went to my local department store and looked for stainless
steel.
I liked the looks, feel, and cost of one new design, and bought
some.
Fifty years later, we still use and like it.
I had chosen a design originally made in Germany called
"Lauffer Design 2."

Later I learned it was displayed in the Museum of Modern Art
in New York.
Now it is very popular and a single fork will sell for $75!

Winter in Chicago

Growing up in an apartment above the stores
At Sheridan Rd. and Irving Park
Winter in Chicago
Icicles on the window panes
Snow on the back porch and work bench
The thermometer is way below freezing.
The grassy yard is covered with snow.
My father's rose bushes lie asleep
Under their blanket of hay,
To sleep until spring.

Women from the 32 apartments
Wash their clothes in the basement as usual,
But hang them there as well.
In the summer, women hung their clothes to dry
On a line over the grassy lawn.
No one hangs them there now.

It's Chanukah time. My father takes his black Chevrolet
Out of one of only four garages off the alley.
We drive from the North side to the South side
Where four sisters in my cousin's family
Have prepared a traditional dinner
With potato latkes, of course, and apple sauce.
Their father is very orthodox
And his blessings are all in Hebrew.

New Year's morning.
We huddle under the blankets
Around our little black and white TV
And watch the Rose parade.
We marvel at the floats
With none of the pretty girls wearing coats,
And the band walking on sunny ground.

We were one mile from Lake Michigan
And I often walked there,
Sometimes with Rosemary,
A young girl from another building.
We'd walk through the snow and ice
And throw stones to skip onto the lake.

I went back once after I was grown.
The apartments were still there,
But the garages were gone.
The lawn and garden were gone
And the space was a parking lot for cars.

Sixty years later Ruth and I are living
In sunny Southern California.
We were married after Thanksgiving 50 years ago
And went to Yosemite on our honeymoon.
We have grown children now.
We saw the Rose Parade in person many years ago.

November and December bring parties and friends.
We celebrate my birthday and our anniversary.
There are the yearly parties,
Our neighbors' party in the cul de sac,
Ruth's Bar Association luncheon,
Her law office's party,
Our Pacific Community of Cultural Jews
Chanukah party, our Cousins Club
of Jews, Palestinians and others
Working for peace in the Middle East.
All happening in sunny weather
With my three rose bushes still in full bloom!

Chicago Autumn

I was blessed with Lake Michigan within a mile of my house.

There were many parks with some trees along the lakefront.

But it wasn't called "the windy city" for nothing

and the trees lost their leaves in a jiffy.

Many autumns I remember my dad driving us

to the Morton Arboretum just 25 miles west of Chicago.

It was filled with trees and trails among them.

In September, October, or November, it was filled with visitors

hiking or riding bikes and enjoying the colorful leaves and

fresh air.

Some people say a man is made outa mud—
well a poet's got nothing but words in his blood:
nouns and verbs 'stead of skin and bone,
add a comma or two, and then he's done.

I was born one mornin' when the sun didn't shine,
so's I picked up a pencil and writ down a line.
Didn't have no paper but a toilet roll,
and the wet nurse said, "Well, bless mah soul!"

I wrote up sixteen rolls and what'd I get?
Another day older and ain't done yet!
Saint Peter, don'cha call me 'cause I ain't got time
to go nowhere's else till I finish my rhyme.   *–Hank Smith*

He Won Her Heart

He won her heart one fine Spring day—
her eyes, her hands, her lips she gave to play.

So long a time for love—
her child, her girl, her woman's mystery way.

She gave him daughtersons
and motherloved them night and day.

He won her heart again, they say,
in age and sorrow, sad and gray,
till life and love a-gone away.

End of Gunfightin'

Chapter I

Old bad Bascomb come ridin' into town
lookin' for Wild Bill, gunfighter renown.

He pokes his head in the old saloon,
says, "Wild Bill, meet me at noon

for a shootout, if you do so dare—
the fastest gun'll live, fair 'n square!"

Outside, they was no birds flyin'
'ceptin' a buzzard lookin' fer the dyin'.

Bad Bascomb drawed first,
but come up with air!

He said, "Whar's mah six-shooter?
Ah knew it'us there!"

Wild Bill sez, "Ah'm old but still fast.
Ah swiped your six-shooter when you went past.

Now gunslingin' in the West is come to an end,
so come on inside an' have a drink with a friend."

And the only shot that'us heerd that day
wuz a shot of Jack Daniels—up an' away.

Chapter II

Bad Bascomb left town, but was he changed?
Nah—he stewed about it till he got deranged!

As a gunfighter, his life'd become a big mess,
so he hijacked a stage of the Pony Express,

loaded his six-shooter, for he was a-grievin'
to find Wild Willie and fight to get even.

So he cracked the whip, made the horses run,
and roared into town with the noonday sun.

The folks in town looked up at the stage,
and Bascomb hollered out in a rage:

"Whar's Wild Willie, that consarned joker?"
A kid said, "He's in the saloon playin' poker."

"Go git him, young'un—tell him Bascomb is here—
and wantin' revenge for bein' insulted last year!"

Bascomb stood high on the coach—like a king on a throne.
Soon Willie came out, walkin' alone

and said to Bascomb, "You barge into town, break up my game.
Gunslingin's over now, so what is your claim?"

Bascomb said, "That's the last card game you'll ever play—
you swiped my six-shooter back then, now you're gonna pay!"

Willie said, "You been drivin' them horses too long, I think,
it's time to get 'em some water to drink

"and gunslingin's over—that's a fact that is true
If you don't believe it, I got one word for you!"

Bascomb looked down. "My word is DRAW!
Gimme your word—or shut up your jaw!"

Willie yelled, "GIDDY-YAP!" and the horses bolted.
The wagon and Bascomb were fiercely jolted.

Bascomb was flipped head under feet,
landed on his backside down on the street.

His six-shooter spun up and went through the air
and was caught by a kid who gave it to Willie right there.

Willie said, "Bascomb, come back on inside—
I'll have to buy another drink for your ornery old hide."

A Barroom Tale

I was packing off the steamer at me good old hometown
port
and off to see me sweetheart, a-ready now to court,

when I see a rowdy party a-down by Selkirk Pier.
So's I vasted that-away and washed by something queer.

T'was an old and wrinkled fishwife, bleary-eyed and pale,
askin wi' her palm out—for a dime to buy an ale.

So's I pressed a buck into her scaly withered hand,
and she gave me a wink, sayin', "My, ain't you just grand!"

Then she beckons me to come along her side
and points to a musty sea-shack by the shoreline tide.

"Dearie," she says, "come a-walkin' wi' me,
an' ye'll get a reward for your charity!"

She seized me arm with a Vulcan grip
an' pulled me along at a devilish clip.

We entered her shack by a narrow door,
an' her tattered shawl dropped to the floor.

A flash of her hand across her face,
an' the grime-salt vanished without a trace.

She whisked off her rags, herself to display,
and I gaped—to behold fair Salomè.

Her hair jet-black, eyes bright blue,
cheeks of a rose-red lusty hue,

she wore but her shimmering seventh veil,
and her motions erected me mast for t'sail.

Some music played an orient piece—
and I, like Jason, espying her fleece—

as her supple arms entranced the air,
she drew me down in a rip-tide snare.

*   *   *   *   *   *   *

The early light when I awoke,
me pledge to me darlin' sweetheart broke,

I glanced at Salomè beside me in bed,
an' I saw in her place the old fishwife instead,

No longer fresh, succulent, fair,
but grizzled wi' brine-crust an' seaweed hair,

she leered wi' one eye, an' a hand to me reached,
and with a foul breath, like a seagull she screeched,

"O stay wi' me, sailor, me earthen child,
an' by me love be e're beguiled."

"Nay, nay, evil hag!" I said and arose
from her kelp-ridden bed and fetched me old clothes.

Yea—old an' marsh-dewed, me suit was decayed
as if in a death-tomb it had o'erlong stayed.

Once away from her door, I turned to look back,
and saw beach-dunes and seabirds, but nowhere the
shack!

Gone too were the pier an' me boat an' the port!
The beach looks now like a sea-side resort.

*   *   *   *   *   *   *   *

So I come to your tavern, to beg of you, sir,
for a drink and some knowledge of what did occur.

"Old-timer," he says, as he pours me a drink,
"that pier was stormed down last century, I think."

"Old-timer, ye call me! I'm not but nineteen—
I come a-shore for m'sweetheart, who I ha' not yet seen."

He points to the mirror, an' in it I gaze.
Lookin' back at me is the Ancient of Days!

Then he pours me another and speaks to me low:
"There's an old legend here—of evil and woe—

that the she-devil Lillith, Adam's first wife,
was the bane of young sailors seeking a life.

She'd guile them and trap them, and be a true whore,
and they'd wake up aged a century yore.

Many a sailor has wandered in here,
fresh from her arms, yet aged and sere,

bereft of their youth and sweethearts and life
from loving a demon—nay, the Devil's own wife.

Instead of a home-lass with a faithful true way,
lured by the flesh of a false Salomè,

they'd unveiled their souls to the red marrow bone
and forfeit their life to the Devil's Old Crone."

*   *   *   *   *   *   *   *

So I leave the barroom, a-shufflin' low,
at the end o' me days, wi' nowhere to go.

But I say to all lads, I say, "Hear! Hear!
Ne'er gie a fishwife a buck for a beer!

Toss her a dime, an' be on your way,
lest she trances your heart as the fair Salomè

an' the life that God gie ye is gone by the morn,
and ye've naught but old age and alone and forlorn."

Wine—A Prose Poem

For wine to be drunk, it first must be artfully poured.

Then, to begin to know its essence, one may gaze at it

through the clearness of the glass. Of course, it must

be smelled with a deep nasal inhalation. One should

drink—as little as possible, as a clever thief stealing a

rare jewel—but drink often, for even a thief must

live—for the history, culture, soil, sun, rain, lay and

slope of the vineyard, the vintner's art—all are

sensed, as if the wine would carry you into another

dimension of taste and into the mystery of the sweet

purpose of Earth undefiled by war and woe.

Herb is a ninety year old retiree who has reached that stage in life where his body is unsupple, his mind is unreliable, his youth is unretrievble and he has become more aware of his bowels than of his genitals.

-Herb Stewart

Someone Like You

Though I am old and bent a bit

I still am here, not out of it

I still am touched when a song bird sings

I still await what each day brings

And when it brings someone like you

There's only one thing I can do

Pursue, pursue

Pursue, pursue

We still should take what we can get

"Cause Glory Be", we ain't done yet

A Question for My Cardiologist

When she's near my heart beat races

Is it from her lissome graces

Or is this strange sensation

Just atrial fibrillation?

I'll Paint You in the Morning Light

I'll paint you in the morning light

Not in the shadows of the night

Your hair soft on the pillow spread

Your fragrance rising from the bed

I'll watch you as you wake and then I'll see

You turn your head and smile at me

I'll paint you as you used to be.

I Know You're in There Somewhere

I know you're in there somewhere

The you that once was you

Deep inside you're hiding there

The you that once I knew

I see a faint light in your eyes

I reach for it in vain

It lives a moment then it dies

And you are gone again

I know not what it's like for you

In that place you've gone to stay

What things you see what things you do

But I ache for yesterday.

To A Wife with Alzheimer's

How can I say what I want you to know

Words left unsaid, I saw part of you go

How can I say what I want you to hear

Words long put off, thought you'd always be here

The words I say now have no meaning for you

It's too late to say them, they cannot get through

I just want to hold you and shout to the sky

Look at us! Look what we did, you and I

But maybe it's me who has lost his own way

Maybe it's me after all who's to say

Maybe I'm here in my own twisted space

Maybe I'm the one trapped in this nightmarish place.

Sleepless

At last at last the morning light

Is pulling up the shades of night

Through all this night I've fitfully

Waited for this time to be

I've tossed and turned and tried in vain

To find the off-switch in my brain

Instead of less its pace is greater

I stepped on its accelerator.

My Pants

When I was young my waist circumference

Was such that I could proudly wear my pants

Stylish and secure around my middle

A picture of good health, fit as a fiddle

But sadly as my years and pounds have got on

I wear them now below my belly button

Pretty Girls

I still love to look at the pretty girls

With their eager eyes and their golden curls

But the rush once felt is there no more

So what am I still looking for

It's like when I am looking at

A lovely painting knowing that

I'll never travel to that place

Or place a soft kiss on that face

And still that warm glow wells in me

At the things I am allowed to see.

Thought I Had It All Down Pat

I thought I had it all down pat

Knew ev'ry this and ev'ry that

Minded all my P's and Q's

Kept up with the latest news

Wore Jeans pants

With nonchalance

Worked my way out of the box

Wore slip-ons without my sox

Set my hat atilt my brow

Lived my life e'er in the now

Grew a one day stubble too

Drove a bee-em-double-yew

And still you never saw me there

Never ran your fingers through my hair

Or whispered sweet things in my ear

Or held my hand and called me dear

And so I find I am without

Those charms you gave another lout.

Mother Spit

Often in my childhood days

My mother in her motherly ways

Would lick a finger daintily

And press it hard but lovingly

Upon a lock of stubborn hair

That kept on lifting in the air

Or sometimes too when I was little

She'd damp a hankie with her spittle

To rub dirt spot off my face

Until of dirt there was no trace

But leaving there instead

A spot real clean but red

I don't know nor can I tell

If mothers now do that as well

If they don't perhaps they would

If at department stores they could

Easily and quickly git

Packaged jars of Mother Spit.

My Love Is Like a Garden Hose

My love is like a garden hose

See how it gushes and it flows

When you return from where you've gone

And come back home and turn me on

A Love Song

I saw you standing there looking lonely

And I wished you were waiting for me

But I knew if I called you would only

Smile and say that it never can be

Oh I wanted to tell you I miss you

To enfold you, to hold you, to kiss you

And I know these are dreams

That will never come true

But I'll never stop wanting them to

No I'll never stop wanting them to.

Remembering a 40's Date

Washed my car 'cause maybe

I'll be pickin' up my baby

Splashed on shaving lotion

Just in case she has a notion

To smile her smile so tender and so sweet

And slide in close against me on the seat

And later when we go

To see a movie show

And I slyly lay my arm across the top part of her seat

And my heart is racing at a rapid breakneck beat

She will turn and nicely fall into my trap

And I'll spill my Coca Cola in her lap.

Thoughts About Growing Old

At times it's very hard to know

If you should stop or you should go

If you should step a different dance

And give yourself another chance

Or just lie down and say, I'm done

So long guys, ain't it been fun

Wait. This can't be my final text

I've got to see what happens next.

Poetry as a medium for creative expression has had a transforming effect upon my life. I am not who I was as a married busy father and Pediatrician. Life gave me the card of widower and finally by choice retiree. That was not an end, but a beginning to explore and discover another life and another me. Poetry was a vehicle of transport from the former to the  present. When a poem resonates with others it reaches a level of intimate connectivity and a familial sense of belonging with others. Then it dawns upon you as you give a poem and receive a poem, you are creating a network of new sisters and brothers. I sense that the poems I write come through me, not from me. There is a spiritual quality I cannot explain. I just know I feel it and am grateful for it.

-Michael Sultan MD FAAP (Ret)

Suddenly Old and Alone

That's the choice, to sit and brood
Or seek another kind of good
New life alone can seem so strange
Until you sense the awesome range
Of new choices and unique voices
That sets imagination burning
You're embarked on a journey
Of growth and learning

It is no folly to be in OLLI
It has become your neighborhood
The spot for being understood
With friends and places
And familiar faces
There's laughter once again

Songs and films, poems recited
Once again you are excited
About each coming day
From first to last, when some have passed
You know that you belong

It's being part of joint tradition
Sharing and caring our recognition
Of all we give and take
Having a piece of the common stake
Blesses our lives with richer meaning

My Fervent Wish

No one comes for me anymore
I sit alone on the shelf of life
Where are the young hands
That reached up and searched for me
In giggling anticipation and with joyful shouts?

I analyze why I am so depressed
No longer am I necessary
In my still obscure existence
Time is dusty and endless
This is my fate
The fate of obsolescence

I am your once beloved roller skate key

Oh how I wish for all of my children of the past
To come together, just one more time,
Now as wizened seniors
Locking our skates upon aged feet
And holding wrinkled hands
For one final, momentous, celebratory
Surging promenade of pride and unified will
Down our well remembered tenement streets
For the last glorious dance
Into the setting sun of the universe.

The Past is Always with Us

Then and Now
Partitioned in my brain
Spilt screen images
Side by side
Each detailed and resonating with feeling
The Jersey City of my boyhood past
Adjacent to the Fullerton Arboretum
Of this gentle sunny morning
The former, a drab assemblage of brick tenements
Juxtaposed and resonating cold, cruel indifference
The symbolic representation
Of loneliness and despair
The Arboretum, abundant with sunshine,
Color and variation
Teeming with life and vibrancy
A cool comforting breeze embraces my soul
A welcoming into the family of existence
Each breath filled with nourishing oxygen
Awakening my senses to all things around me
To possibility
To aliveness
To creativity surging within
I am
I am alive!
Gratitude envelops me like a cape
I wear it with pride and deep appreciation
For my emancipation from the past
And into what matters in the present.

The Wind

If you are a sailor
It makes you subservient
Without it, your sails are useless
And you cannot move your craft

Across a snowy open plain
It is a sculptor, shaping a new landscape
Or it may be the undertaker
Burying what it wishes

When the air is hot and still
You crave it as a lover
When it roars too loudly
It awakens you from sleep

If it decides to twist circumferentially
It fascinates
Then it destroys all
That lies in its chosen forward path

When it embraces the windmill
Water moves
And electricity flows
And when it is incessant
You crave
The silent stillness

As it rips away the shingles
Overturns furniture
And smashes windows
You sense its capacity for maniacal rage

When it cools your hot, sweaty body
You feel its compassion and understanding
When it makes your kite soar crazily
It invokes triumphant jubilation

It is present when it chooses
It cannot be packaged or bottled
And it cannot be seen with your eyes
It detests only the inventors
And users of fans and jets
Whose products it regards
As souless imposters
Of its godly might and will

Dreamwork

In my sleep all logic falls away
All freed up to seek or play
From the residue of this very day
Conflicts and problems or hidden slights
Am I gearing up to fight?
The things that threaten and give me fright
Or imagined moments that bring delight
Cast aside those earthly shackles
There is no challenge you cannot tackle

Later on when you're awake
You conclude a different take
Every part of dreams is what you make
One is coping for your own sake
Wrestling in sleep you are a dancer
Seeking for the final answer
For problems in life you did not solve
In your sleep ignite resolve
To block some thrust and then to parry
Should I be single or choose to marry?

In that unconscious theatre of your mind
You can envision what had been blind
Indulge your lust or kill some swine
You make the rules of every kind
Speak to the dead or travel through time
To places from so long ago
Where you found beloved friends and hated foe
Then daylight comes and you must go
Where reality, not you, defines all that which is truly so

Your two worlds awake or not
So many dreams you have forgot
In each one there is a plot
Forever you'll seek that safety spot
Read about Jung, heard about Freud
It leaves one feeling so annoyed
You created a spontaneous production
And they have made their own deduction
But it was you who made the whole construction
Producer, actor, fool or king
In the dream you are all those things

Day of Emancipation

An ocean of asphalt
A sea of brick
Dark shadows abound
Joyless, only the hum of vehicles
Tenement windows speak of separation
Of walls, between, alongside, below and above
The plant of depression flourishes here.
Sporadic outbursts of violence
And ugly sounds of despair

But today is different!
You stand at the shoreline
Water tickles your pleasured feet
Partially submerged in the sand
The sun shines brightly, and
Its rays creep into your soul
The horizon is vast
Loudly speaking of endless possibility

A gentle breeze caresses all of you
With a delicious intimacy
Reminding you how starved you have been
For light
For love
For touch
For hope

With each crashing wave
And your jubilant immersion
Hearing your own unrestrained laughter
You are being transformed
By your unbridled happiness
Yes, yes
Born again! Born again!

Poetry Class Meets At Marcia's House

Beyond the rhymes
Beyond the verse
Beyond the turn of a phrase
Beyond the masters of long ago
Beyond the delight with ingenious new poems
It is this "thing" we have together

More than camaraderie
More than an ambience of good humor
More than being heard
More than expressing one's self
It is our unspoken agreement
To travel together
Without moving an inch

Into a world of endless possibility
That is not limited
By the rules or traditions
Of earthly decorum
In that world
Even flowers can speak
And we can choose to engage the deceased
Once again

Priorities

Not to spend a moment, a precious moment on regret
Or fear of death
Or planning for some distant future
Ingest each moment like a delicacy
Like a gift, like the privilege it is
Now is everything
Finding magic in the ordinary
The taste of warm bread
The emerging sun
The cool wind of relief
The cold rain nourishing your plants
Even pain has value
As you quickly retract your hand
From the hot stovetop

Loss brings into awareness the riches you held
That were taken for granted
When I enjoy the dance, the joke, the loving
I hope that I am modeling
To my children and their children
That it is not work OR play
But work AND play
Being open is such a winning strategy
One is infused by the things and thoughts
Of others unlike yourself, who enrich your existence

Knowledge alone is not wisdom
I will try to be more like my late beloved wife
Understanding that it is futile to try to be loved
The task is to be loving

After spending his "youth-in-asia",

Sam came to the US from India for graduate studies, getting his MS in Environmental Engineering from UCI, and his MBA in Finance from UCLA. After working in these two fields, Sam is exhilarated to be at OLLI, where he says he is discovering his artistic and his touchy-feely side, which he never thought ha had! He is thrilled to be trying his hand at music, ceramics, theatre – and poetry, in the two years he has been at OLLI.

Sam says he is beginning to love Poetry. Shakespeare's Sonnets give him the utmost satisfaction, as he loves reciting them in an exaggerated version of his sing-song Indian accent, using which he thinks can master a Sonnet's Iambic Pentameter rhyme.

-Sam Sumanth

"Gold On Mars"

JPL's Mars explore, Curiosity, landed flawlessly on Mars
while the London 2012 Olympics were on.

Happiness is what you feel,
When you win a race and take gold.
But ecstasy is what everyone feels,
When Curiosity lands on Mars.

The noble lesson we take from this
It's best when all are winners!
There's only one winner in an Olympic race,
While everyone is a winner at the JPL.

Empathy

Do you really feel the other's pain
Or is it all for show?

Can you really be in the other's shoes
And feel their heartfelt woes?

Will you really do some noble good,
Or keep going your selfish way?

No Space For Birds

Two birds, they fly over the globe
Looking for clean air to breathe
Man has destroyed this lovely planet
With greed, greed and more greed!

Where will they fly, what will they do
With no place to breed, and no place to go
Will they simply die up in the sky
Another symbol of our irreversible pollution?

Love Story

They say you are average
But I alone can see
That glow that resides
Deep inside you.

You are beautiful and enchanting
You are simply fascinating
I love your coy pouting and sulking
That tortures my heart's pounding.

There is so much life
In all you do
You laugh, you cry
You flood me with passion!

Soft as a breeze
Hot as lava
That glow inside you
Sets me afire.

You smile, you tease
You fake so much anger
But I know deep down
Passionate for me you are.

Your love starts deep down
From your noble, giving soul
It rises through your heart,
Which is more than pure gold.

Never did I need
A body so close
Each and every moment
Deep in my soul.

Your warmth, your laughter
The kindness in you
My heart you slaughter
My very breath you are!

I love you my darling
There is no more I can say.

Yoda, My Love

My little Yoda, I loved her so much
Ugly-Cute like ET, a darling she was
Chuweeni was the name they gave her
Half Chihuahua and half Weenie.

 From morning till night, wag she did
Her big little tail, from side to side
A smile she always had on her face
A grin she had, if all you said was hi.

People she just loved
Dogs she mostly snubbed
But only after she gave them
A patronizing little rub.

Friendly from her heart she truly was
And so thoroughly lovable
All four times that she was lost
Each time she had a visitor's ball.

She ended up a welcome guest
With the first person that saw her
Because whoever saw her said
This funny looking dog, she's simply the best!

Ugly-Cute she surely was
But so very adorable
That one and all, they simply thought
She was oh so pretty and lovable.

After many a dog in her family,
 Between her sisters and her mother
Yoda was the first pup ever
My wife, she ever loved!

She talked, she played, she suffered her pains
She surely fell for Yoda
She chatted, she played, she hugged her tight
And she even got her in a cuddle!

So now she knows the heartbreak
That made me sob and sob
Each time I lost a doggie friend
So many a time in the past!

Well, little Yoda, rest in peace
Beautiful love of mine
That last lovely look on thy little face
Tells me you've gone to heaven.

Amen, my little Angel Yoda
May your soul rest in peace
Heartbreak you have given me
You grinning little E.T.!

War, O' Glorious War

When I look at you, my darling boy,
Lying there lifeless and wasted
I feel so guilty for my gutless silence
Just standing by when they sent you to war.

    Much civilized we think we are
    Ten fold more since Hannibal
    Yet still we want to keep on killing
    In war after war.

Looking at your body now
So very ashamed I be
So callously we sent you to kill
On one pretext or another.

We brainwash you and order you
To kill all who think not like you
Wise thinkers we think we are
Yet we fathom not why different they think

What we really want is to kill them all
Each one of them who think not like us
For then all alive will think alike
And peaceful we think we'll be.

But after the war when all alive
Now say they think like you and me
Kill, kill, kill, we tell you again
Kill all who look different than you.

Kill freely and with abandon, Soldier
All your bravery from home we'll see
So much fun it is on TV
Cheering for you and priding ourselves.

So keep on fighting O' soldier of mine
All the spoils of war we'll share with you
But if you do not return home,
We know our share is even more.
Sorry we'll say. We simply are.

Our God is a great savior we believe,
And pious we think we are.
Yet in that same God's name we kill
Saying my God is superior.

If victorious, we return home with our gun
To kill people manically in our town
We kill creatures that crawl fly or run
We're the only species that kills for fun.

My Peace

I searched for ever inside my soul,
For the happiness within me.

I searched afar for miles and miles
For things that would make me happy
Then one from the Buddha's life
Wisdom and enlightenment I got.

I cannot tell you how it came,
I cannot teach you whence it came.
I can only say, self-taught it was
For wisdom truly dwells in thee.

Buddha in the east, Kant in the west,
They shone the light for us to see
The truth is neither East nor West
It is simply plain universal.

What's good for you, only you will know
By looking deep inside your soul
Your clean mind and pure soul will let you know
Whatever it is you need to know.

What happens happens want it or not
Just accept it and detach yourself
Because life is what happens to you
While for it you are planning.

So do not wait for tomorrow
It's wise to be content with today
For there is happiness in every day
If you will only let it come your way.

So all I tell you in the end my friend
No words of wisdom I can teach
Knowledge you can get from gurus and books
But wisdom is what will come from within.

You have no choice but to live your day
Whatever it may bring
Good or bad your soul will tell
So pine not for things you do not have.

Live the life that you feel is right
Right or wrong, your spirit will tell
If it's right it's right, if it's wrong it's wrong
You will know from deep within your heart.

What is right for me can be wrong for you
What gives me peace may give you war
Only your soul can tell you right or wrong,
If you will simply listen to it!

No one can tell you what you want
No one can tell you what makes you happy
Remember you are the master of your fate
And the captain of your soul.

When I was once pressed to write my autobiography in exactly six words, I promptly wrote: "My mind is always playing hopscotch!" I'm not alone; this is probably true of at least half of our OLLI members, and probably at least seventy-five percent of our "Poetry for Pleasure" group. We spur each other on - we are an eclectic bunch who enjoy each other immensely. Although I have a Masters Degree, I will never earn a doctorate because membership in OLLI is a dilettante's dream!

–Betty Tang

Basic Training

Somewhere between inoculation shots
And the Army's thou shalt nots,
Between being gassed,
Endless sit-ups,
And two-mile runs,
Reality sets in.

Drill Instructors know it's those
Who can embody—
Not just memorize—
"The Seven Army Values"
Who will win their own
Self-respect, and that of others.

The Seven Army Values?
Loyalty, Duty, Respect,
Selfless Service, Honor,
Integrity, and Personal Courage.

Wait a minute!
Aren't these values we should all embrace?

Grandma's Matryoshka Doll

There she stands,
smiling from across the room.
She is dressed for a festive occasion.
Red and blue flowers adorn her dress.
A bright floral scarf covers her head.
How very beautiful she looks today!
Inside she holds a special secret.
Shall I show you what it is?
Yes? Wonderful! Are you surprised
by all those other lovely girls inside her, each one
smaller than the last? Sit beside me, my granddaughter,
so your Babushka can tell you the story of our past, and how
you and your cousins are a special part of our Russian heritage.
I will tell you what these eight lovely Matryoshka Dolls mean to me.
The largest one, who holds the others, is my great, great, grandmother.
She was from a tiny village near Moscow; it's so lovely there my dear.
The second is my great, grandmother; I will show you her picture.
Nesting inside her is my dear Babushka, who I remember so well.
Next comes my mother, who once carried me within her body.
I am number five in our family's precious nesting dolls.
Look, there are three more Matryoshka Dolls left!
Can you guess who is number six of the eight?
Yes, your mother is number six, so you
are number seven of our matriarchal line.
I will buy you your own Matryoshka Doll
then teach you all of our family's names;
because one day you might have a daughter
who would love to hear the story of our family.

I'm An American, Supersize Me!

I'm a big star athlete with money to spend.
I'm gonna buy me the biggest, meanest,
HUMVEE on the planet,
The biggest house with the biggest pool
surrounded by Laker Girls, Dallas Cowgirls,
and a truck full of food from the Cheesecake Factory!
YEAH - Supersize me; I'm an American!
I'm lookin' for the best agent around so I'll be
Mr. Nike on every channel, day and night.
Come on man; don't look at me like that!
I might hire you— IF
you guarantee to supersize me!
What? You dare to criticize me?
You're living just like me on a smaller scale—
A house with twice the mortgage you can afford,
You had the money to buy a Ford,
but chose to lease a Lexus
that you can't even write off!
That was you thumping your chest
thinking, I'm an American, supersize me!
I hear you got engaged recently—
That diamond was so big I'll bet you'll still be
paying for it after the baby comes.
I'll bet she cooed, "Oh come on, Honey, buy me
THAT ring, supersize me!"
Not much chance we'll ever scale down.
Our wants are endemic— in fact, they're epidemic!
Everyone buying and justifying,
"I'm an American, supersize me!"

History's Bell Curve

Many believe
Our country will defeat
the bell curve of history.

By forgetting 9/11
we convince ourselves
that we will have
no more monuments turning
into shattered visages.

Unlike Ozymandias, King of Kings,
our works will not decline.

Some say
not even the four horsemen
of the Apocalypse
could bring us down.

How blind we are to the history -
of the rise and fall of nations!
Wake up! Please wake up,
or are you only
pretending to be asleep?

Listen to me!
Even if all our people were made of iron,
even iron can be destroyed
as it experiences its own corrosion
from within.

Wake up.

Summer Solstice

How life affirming
the rising sun will prove by
sending its arrows of light
through the polyliths of
Stonehenge.
How festive the crowds
that have been here all night.

Drumbeats, drumbeats, pounding,
feverish, hypnotic, reverberations,
arouse the primitive yearnings in us.
Trance like, the crowd sways - unknowingly
dancing with their dead ancestors
throughout the night at Stonehenge.

These ancient stones have
seen and heard all this and more.
They've served witness to
human sacrifice and wars.

In ancient times,
the months between sowing seed
and harvest time
were reserved for war.
The Rites of Summer Solstice
commemorate that painful mittelschmerz.

Ah, for the brevity of those wars,
savage as they were.

If only the narrow beams of light
now piercing Stonehenge
could enlighten and expunge
the savage in us,
how life affirming that would be.

Interpreting Louis Simpson

If you're going to be a writer
Become the shark.
Swallow or spit out indigestible criticism—
Or better yet—
Swallow the critic!
Having a dry spell?
Know that you will (as always)
Write your way out of the desert.

The Rabbit's Proverb

If the rabbit talks,
I've never heard him.
Does he know that many
of his brethren's feet
are someone else's lucky charms?
Perhaps that's why
he keeps his mouth shut.
After all,
"A closed mouth gathers no feet."

Twinkle, Twinkle Little Planet*

Twinkle, twinkle,
Little Planet
too high in the sky—
Damn it!

Proclaimed a diamond
(who would lie)?
To bring some back
I'm sure we'll try.

Twinkle, twinkle,
new space endeavor;
diamonds enough
to last forever!

Their price has fallen—
Supply? demand?
We aren't now rich
the way we'd planned?

Twinkle, twinkle
Little Planet—
who let your secret out?
Damn it!

*National Geographic Daily News, "Diamond Planet Found." Part of a Whole New Class? Carbon-rich exoplanet has chemistry not seen before, astronomers say. (Published October 11, 2012)

On A Hot Day In The City

I saw you on that hot bus, Sister,
hanging onto that pole—
your composure
on its very last nerve!

Sweat and pain shrouded your eyes—
every body knocking
against
every body else!

Then the bus lunges around the corner
hurling you hard!
hard against
that skinny gal!
Guess too much body and age
overrode good sense
'cause when the young gal screamed,
you lit into her!

"You ain't hurt!
You think you so delicate
'cause you so light?
Just shut up that whining!"

Shut my mouth too, Lord.
That poet, Arnold Adoff, was right,
We all need to "Stop
looking and start loving."

What Can I Say Louise?

(The poet, Louise Gluck)

Had to read you for an assignment.
What can I say, Louise?
Best I borrow from Mohammed Ali— you
float like a butterfly and sting like a bee!

Sometimes you ramble like a rose—
sweetly opening petals of vulnerability
only to become one of those man eating plants
a few lines later.

What can I say, Louise?

Wow!

Fritz von Coelln

The confluence of love lost and love gained,
faith questioned and faith renewed have
evolved my purpose in life and inspired my
poetry. I stand with a blocked artery replaced
with collaterals taking up the slack. Humbled
by circumstances and choices, God has given
me a second chance and I accept His challenge.
-Fritz von Coelln

When I Think Of You

And I think of you…
Every ten minutes when I'm awake
In every dream when I'm asleep
In every stirring fantasy
       in every fleeting thought

I think of you…
Holding hands for that first time
Hugging close, tight
Kissing, those little kisses
       in machine gun bursts

I think of you…
Singing, your voice smiling
Praising, your hands reaching high
Praying, your eyes closed
       wiping away a tear

I think of you…
Loving you beyond all others
Reaching for your touch
Yearning for your consent
       your heartfelt smile

Please accept this Christmas gift
In the Victoria's Secret bag
And be assured
I think of you…
       wearing only these….

We Are Two Magnets

North and south poles
creating fields of exhilaration
when we attract
oh, do we attract
when we repel
we do repel.

Yet the forces of attraction
are far greater
than the forces that repel
so we bounce back and forth
hearts racing
breaking
yet, in God's grace
always filled with love.

We hold hands in passion
we hold hands to pray
we hold hands to steady our course
we hold hands as we say good bye
—even for the last time
that, in God's will
we reach out again to touch
oh, that wondrous feeling
just holding hands.

We need each other
yet, we batter our hearts so needlessly.

We pray
to rend our selfish needs
and simply grant each other
to hold each other's hand
delighted by love.

Mustang

He is to be heard: 500 strong, growling
  brawny, sinuous muscle, yellow, screaming yellow
  sleek, solid, sensuous, the Peregrine in flight
He is legendary: Ford, Shelby, Rousch, Shaker,
  Kenne Bell, Brembo, McPhearson, passionate
He is salacious: displacement, torque, cubic inches
  bore, stroke, compression, compulsive
He is reckless: supercharged fast, the cheetah in pursuit
  zero to 60 in 4.5, intoxicating

Trapped on the Interstate, flagged down, tagged!

I too, am to be heard: running alone, trembling
  this dominant stallion rebuffed
  no harem, no mares nor foals: feral, the mesteño
I chase the beauty of the seasons: free-roaming
  the grace of God provides my Western range
I know, I don't understand: Massacre Lakes, Fog Hog,
  Calico Mountain
  opening themselves to me, haven from angst
I am imprisoned: this unbridled freedom,
  these wild plains, grasses brown, wither and die

I, eluding, yet yearning: the lasso, the brand, the fence!

Jersey Shore

If I struggle with the words
is it lack of inspiration
or trepidation of what will come once begun
if I begin at all?

Tediously
a barge scrapes the horizon clean
a straight-curved line
punctured by a jib going south.
The ringing of the ice-cream man's bells
dissipates in the wind.

Culling, the wake dissipates
the grey sea reflects the overcast
the green reflecting the blue sky
hazel in between by eye.

The jelly fish spume
frothing, bubbling
a horrid heart pulsating
thrashing in the wind
incessant wind
southward today
yesterday easterly.

I stand, feet sinking into the sand
the tide rhythms dividing equally
blue to the left
grey to the right
and I ask Him
what is my responsibility in all this?
It is not about me.
It is all about me.

And he rings his bells again
dreadfully into the wind
carrying his quest away.
Easy to listen
to follow
to succumb
the ultimate darkness.

Silently
the screaming
the incessant wind
the thin veil flutters
eventually tatters
unless the surrogate found
the Word, indelibly ingrained.

Yearning
silently screaming .
It is not about me.
It is all about me.
Getting it on so to speak.

The bells
he rings his bells again
the line, blue/grey, unmoving
yet, slowly moving in some direction.

Smile and they will hear it
the chilling wind.

Abomination!
Heaven abounds around me.
Within, the chaos of Hell!

Mea culpa amice!

The Truckin' Devil

The old pickup truck rumbled
'long the dirt road, going somewhere
nowhere in particular
The driver picking out the ruts, rocks
in the dim headlights
The tail lights leaving a soft afterglow
red in the darkness reflecting ghostly
   fence posts, tumble weeds
   the ditch along the side, little else
The truck was, at one time, tan
now rust spots rimmed the wheel wells
mud splotches from last winter's rains
trimmed the running boards, the grill, the wheels
dust covered the hood, windshield, roof, bed

Two straw hats struggled in the bed
the wind whipped one way, then another
up and down, back and forth
A light-blue ribbon band decorated one
ribbon ends fluttering
The other hat with a bandana band once red
now stained with sweat, almost black

Struggling side to side, up and down
the red bandana banded hat floated up and out
reflecting in the reddish glow
disappearing in the darkness
The hat with the light-blue ribbon floated up and out
It too, reflecting, disappearing

At an intersection, two dirt roads going nowhere
the driver, bored with the somewhere, nowhere ride
turned 'round, maneuvering back and forth on the
narrow roads
returning the way he had come
returning back to somewhere

Dim headlights picked up the hat
the one with the light-blue ribbon
Too late, crushed by the right front tire
Stopping, he got out, picking it up
   throwing it into the bed of the truck

A hundred yards later
(although no one was measuring)
he spotted the other hat
the one with the red bandana band
   primly sitting on top of a tumble weed
    at the side of the road
Stopping, getting out, picking it up
   tossing it into the bed
continuing on to somewhere

She rotated the brim in her fingers
pushed out the bowl of the flattened hat
A tear along the intersection of brim and bowl
the light-blue ribbon
   grey with dust
   ground-in dust
The wind whirled around her
her lips tasted of mud, her lungs stung from dust
her eyes...
   A tear fell onto the ribbon
   creating a black splotch!

He placed the hat with the red bandana band
on his head
   low over his eyes
   high in the back
   and grinned!

Flash Rap

Flash!
  1/potato
  2/potato
  3/potato
  4
        Bang!
Flash!
  1/potato
  2/potato
  3
        Bang!
Flash! Flash! Flash!
No/potato
        Bang! Bang! Bang!

Rattle, Rattle, Rattle
Down spouts protest
Clamor in the drainpipes
Out pour the gutters
Clogging in the drains

Signs "NO DUMPING"
"GOES TO THE OCEAN"

With all this babbling, ranting, raving
Why don't the oceans overflow?
For some it's global warming
For some it's earthly sinking
For some…
        Who cares?

Bring on the sunshine
        Let's get it on!

I could not believe it! I was in the top ten percent of those taking the entrance exam for Fullerton College. I was a foreigner without an education and I checked twice at the office to believe my test results. So I took all the hard classes that would allow me to transfer to a university. I continued my charity work, then I restored old houses. Life takes strange twists and brought me back to college (OLLI) at the age of 70 something. I am delighted that three of my grandchildren are enjoying poetry classes.

—Ingrid Werner

Peaceful

In
The
Name
Of
God
We
Kill
Each
Other
For
The love
Of
Country
We
Kill
Each
Other

If
We
Were
Truly
One
Nation
Under
God
Who would be left?

Traveling America Once More

The splendor from fifty years ago still lies over the land
Plentiful and rich
Have my eyes not dimmed
Has my soul not aged
Has the countryside, like myself, remained unchanged
I was a young woman then
Hardly more than a girl
I held high aspirations
And so did the country
Here and there small communities sprang up
That are now good sized cities
When one's soul is young, one's heart is younger yet
From mystical grounds our roots have sprung
We used them daily
Thinking of life then and now
Fearless, I travel as I did when young
Did I then enjoy it more
The reverberation of my soul
Assures me that all is well
And that this trip is as pristine as the first

Moonlit Night

Younger dreamers left their castles in the sand
Most were washed away
Driftwood covered in sand
Barefoot I walk
The pale moon hangs low and wood burns
Down to a few glowing embers
I miss my lover's arm around me
I tell myself again
Love is a reality appearing to the senses rather than the
intellect
And yet I cry for your touch
Powerful and strong the ocean wave kisses the sand
Breaking up into smaller kisses that stretch out their lips
To caress the wet sand—kisses everywhere

My Cowardice (Devastation?)

WW II broke out in Germany, 1939
Atomic bomb-Harry Truman,
Hiroshima and Nagasaki, 1945

I was young when Nazis did horrible things
I wept for New York's Twin Towers
Crying when I saw the giant mushroom-
Turning live people into dripping molasses
Race riots destroyed Los Angeles' façade
And so it goes
How can I
Knowing about what is going on
Do so little

Storms or Winds

No aimless breeze, you little tornado
Stormy as a summer wind
Puffing yourself up with all your might
On rooftops you try to play "tag" at night
Sending umbrellas flying with a toyish tug
Tossing girls skirts up for a boyish mug
"Breezing up" is what fishermen say
Great Gusts? Are you here to stay?
Blowing Sahara sand in my face
As if you could not find any other place
Driving waves of rain through summer
Fields and open plains
At least swing down to Antarctica's snow
There behind the icebergs
Blow, Blow, Blow

Fossil's Wisdom

For
the
last
12 million
years
Above
it
all
Hovering
high
in
the
sky
Way
above
the
clouds
In
silent
beauty
and
ancient
aloneness
God
is goodness and understanding

Emily's Dreams Unlimited

Wild nights, wild nights
Were I with Thee
Wild night should be our luxury
Indifferently I see him yawn
I know
That no hot lips shall be pressed on mine
Unless I choose more dreams divine

I Would Love You More

It's once in a lifetime that such a love comes along
That would rile up the poets to write a new song
It's once in a lifetime there is someone like you
    There is someone like me
If all the clocks of the universe stopped telling time
I would love you as mine
If the earth changed its rhythm of rotation
I'd love you the same
If the water learned to run upwards to the top
I would love you the same, I'd never stop
If ONLY once YOU would say you love me too
I'd love you more
Deeper and stronger than ever before
I'd love you so much they would call it "sick"
Hordes of others would beat me off with a stick
I'd love you till the cows come home
The Florentine Basilica would lift off its dome
That's how our love must be

Real Power

Perhaps art is our only true reflection
Art might be the mirror of our life
It shows us our collective face
Our beauty, the wrinkles, the spots
Mercilessly revealing—
Our Have's and the Have Not's
Art offers in style and dress
How humanity wears its success
Instead of an empowering title or throne
Everyone now has a telephone
We have invented more than we can use
Who's left to worry about the atomic fuse?

For Whom the Trumpet Blows

I have not had an original idea
In way longer than a year
In all the blossoming of spring
I waited for my song to sing
I waited all through the summer
Saw falling leaves and snow
But my mind as always is going
Going-Going-Go
Not one idea not even a used one
Not a new feeling—not even a shmozzed one
Is love a certain mannerism-a look—a voice?
Does the river murmur or is it just noise?
The secret sits in the middle and knows
The one for whom the trumpet blows

Reference:
"But the Secret sits in the middle and knows."
By Robert Frost

Rayleen was encouraged by a friend to join OLLI when she retired. In her second year attending OLLI she discovered the "Poetry for Pleasure" class. It is indeed fun. She didn't even know she liked poetry. Since joining the poetry class she has written over 50 poems, and is in the process of illustrating them. She plans to bind them into a book to share with her family and friends. Most of her poetry tends to focus on an animal or some aspect of nature.

–Rayleen Williams

Last Day of Summer

Red and orange ripples rise, sink, waver,
Across the blue and liquid ocean surface,
From horizon to shore,
Directing vision to eternity
And yet touching this moment—
Reflections of an orb
Marking the last day of summer.

Silhouetted against the moving spectrum,
A slight and slender boy rushes out to sea,
Following the retreat of waves
That have just washed the sandy beach.
Then, splashing
Towards shore,
He races ahead
Of falling waves
That collapse around
His ankles and knees,
The foam flattening and
Spreading across the sand.

The silhouette jumps and leaps,
Frolicking in the blaze
Of light and liquid—
The joy of life and future.
Pausing, curious, he digs
At bubbles breaking
Through the wet sand,
Grabbing an escaping crablet,
Then turning, bending, to select pieces of shells—
Remnants of unknown shattered lives.
And, in a moment, he's off chasing sea gulls,
Gliders that skim wave crests
Or touch the sand at his toes,
Trying to snatch the crablet from his fingers.

All this—a memory or a dream of youth?
Hope once danced in the dark and widened pupils
Of the man whose hand I hold,
Who breathes lightly in shallow whispers,
On this last day of summer.
Too soon, a year cut short,
A year missing fall and winter.

Domesticated

Silver colored red fox
Runs wild in Siberian woods,
Captured, kenneled, tamed.

Submissive pups kept,
Bred; their submissive pups kept,
Selective breeding.

Hormones altered, changed,
Physiology reacts,
Domesticated.

Barking, wagging tails,
Broad skulls, whimpering, whining.
Juvenile traits held.

More, and more dog-like,
Eager for human contact,
Friendly, like to please.

Compliant manners,
Calm temperament chosen,
Aggression suppressed.

Color changed—spotted,
White, mottled coats; tails held high,
No longer wild fox.

Friendly fox puppies,
Tamed in ten generations.
Wild fox now trained dog.

Human ancestors,
Tribal hunters, gatherers,
Cooperative.

Social ties are strong,
Face to face interactions,
Communication.

Agriculture grows,
Industrial Revolution,
Machines do human work.

Muscles atrophy,
Weakened physiology,
Lighter body frame.

Computers—brain work,
Replacing cellular brain,
Thinking diminished.

Smart phones—text, tweet, twit—
Social contact without touch,
Senses blunted, lost.

Blank stares at blue light,
Hand held electronic card,
True faces ignored.

Expression, eyes— gone,
Electronic dependency,
Brain smaller, shrinking.

Privacy dissolved,
Non-thinking isolation,
Captured, kenneled, tamed.

Hormones altered, changed,
Physiology reacts,
Domesticated.

Hand in Hand

Between my toes, wet sand,
Suspended in the wash of spent waves,
Records each step I take,
Then dissolves with the repeating tongues of sea.

Hand in hand my daughter walks with me,
My large prints, her small impressions,
Each indenting the sand, then edges smoothed,
Prints flattened, enlarged,
Disappearing in the wash of water.

Each life leaves footprints, track ways,
That say, "I was here."
Too soon, too quickly, most dissolve, evaporate,
Before even the trail is complete.

Yet, some stories are caught, frozen in time,
Such are the track ways of the Paluxy River.
Stone prints tell a narrative of past and foreign lives.
These prints, too, formed along a beach
Washed by the tongues of sea water.

Hand in hand my daughter walks with me
Following the stone prints of the Paluxy,
Those ancient three-toed prints, so large,
My daughter pauses to sit in one.

Our muddy footprints dissolve in the gentle river flow
Before we've taken five steps more; yet, the life story
Of these past giants have remained 113 million years,
And now we ponder, explore,
Imagine times, lives otherwise unknown.

Two kinds of giants passed this way—
Three-toed tracks flank more rectangular prints,
This is the style of predator following prey.
What caught time and held this moment?

We are told calamity overtook them all.
Volcanic ash, hot, molten, fell on this ancient path,
Fusing sand, hardening instantly by the touch of cold sea,
Forever holding the mold
Of this past day and moment.

Hand in hand my daughter walks with me.
What track way will we leave for time?
Hand in hand I, we, walk
With all the sons and daughters across all the seas.

Must we face calamity
To have our story, our life, kept and held;
But if catastrophe rains down, who will there be
To read the story of our impressions,
Large and small, along the wash of sea?

Feline Musings

There she sits upon her throne,
Still, contained, content to be alone.
Her eyes look with clarity and intent,
Definitely piercing and intelligent.

What exactly are her thoughts?
There are no words to reveal her plots.
She patiently watches out,
Surveying with confidence and clout.

We humans with our narcissistic view,
Cannot consider intellect of any other hue.
So she sits and waits,
Silently musing at our contradictory traits.

lace

bent over and holding tight
her head is turned down
in what inward place
and out of sight
is she contemplating
or is this a wall built
'round her space
seeking grace
from mortared guilt
holding brick and
broken bit
in jumbled patterns
that do not fit
or is the pull
of inward sorrow
tying losses
of the past
and tomorrow
within her
curled and
tensing form
where is
the entrance
for hope
to warm
and open her
folded arms
to embrace
and wrap her
in the delicate
variations
of life's lace?

Whose light—

Whose light this is
I think I know,
His house is in
My heart and soul.

He no longer
Is aware
That I silently watch
The wind blow bare—

The branches
Of the forest trees,
And stand among
The gathering leaves.

I hope that
It is true,
Spring will bring
Life buds anew.

But now I can only
Dream and wait,
Wondering if green births
Can change my fate.

Served in USNR, two years in the South Pacific in World War 2.
Received PhD at University of Southern California. Co-authored <u>A</u>
<u>Teacher is</u> <u>Many Things</u>, Published by Indiana University Press and
translated into 26 languages for circulation throughout the world.
Founder of the Department of Theatre and Dance, Cal State Fullerton
Served as Chair of the department for nine years.
Associate Vice-President for Academic Programs, Cal State Fullerton
In charge of curriculum development for all the colleges of the
university for eleven years.
Member of the Founding Committee for The Muckenthaler Center.
President, Rotary Club of Fullerton, 1981-1982
Governor of Rotary International District 5320 (66 clubs in Orange
County and East Los Angeles county) 1985-1986
Since 1991 he and Dottie, his spouse, have traveled to many part of
the world presenting a one-man show depicting the life of the founder
of rotary.
President of the Emeriti Association (Retired Professors of Cal State
Fullerton) for five years.
Continues to raise funds for the university and other philanthropic
recipients in the Fullerton area.
Charter president of the Mamm Alliance for the support of The
Performing Arts at Cal State Fullerton. At CSUF
First Faculty member to be named "Honorary Alumnus" at CSUF
Published poems in several anthologies
Volunteer in "Poetry for Pleasure" class at "OLLI" at Cal State
Fullerton.   *–Jim Young*

Tamed by a Scrub Jay

Ready at your beck and call, I hear your Scrub Jay
squawking pierce the reddening dawn.
From my window I can see you perched on eaves,
demanding my appearance.
"Come out to play and don't forget the peanuts",
Is how I hear your early morning screech.
Could I be wrong about "the play"?
Perhaps the peanuts would suffice.

Fearing that impatience might cause you to seek new
playmates,
I grab unsalted peanuts from a jar and softly step outside
the sliding door.
Lifting my open palm towards your cherished confidence.
I wait the gentle prickling of your tiny feet on fingers you
have come to know
That will not harm you.

Grasping with your needle claws and ruffling wings for
balance,
You cock your head in triumph. You have given
commands.
You have been obeyed.

Before dipping for a nut, knowing full well I will
replenish the supply
You fill your beak in hurried pecks
Then triumphantly you dive toward the gravel walkway
Trusting me to help you keep the secret,
You lay the nuts aside and rapidly bob storage
Where you bury your treasure, each one, carefully
Gravel by gravel, storing them for another day when
winter comes
—if it comes.

Spellbound, I wait with open palm
While you skip, hop, dip, flutter, cover,
Triumphantly taking your time to store your food
Before your arrogant return to the willing slave who
conquered
Your confidence and trust.

Mouse

I got a birthday present.
It was a little mouse.
I kept him in a little cage
Which was his little house.

I always liked to make him play
So I could pull his tail.
I thought it funny when he squealed
Inside his little jail.

He never had to hunt for food.
I'd feed him now and then.
I didn't know he needed more
Till I saw him getting thin.

He didn't have a playmate
Except for Joey and me,
So sometimes he got lonely
When we did other things you see.

His cage was short and he got long.
He couldn't play and run.
So he slept much more than he really
Should instead of having fun.

Why Pardon a Thanksgiving Turkey?

The president pardoned a turkey.
Now what did the turkey do?
Why did he need to be pardoned?
He was willing to feed me and you!

He was willing to have his head lopped off
He was willing to find himself plucked
He was willing to lie on the table
With his legs up because he'd been stuffed.
He was happy to be surrounded
By people with forks and knives
To lop off his legs, to carve up his chest
So they could enjoy their lives.

Well, turkeys don't need to be pardoned.
They need your blessing instead
Because they mean a lot more to you
When they lie on your table dead.

Surround them with stuffing and gravy.
Add biscuits and veggies galore...
Mint jelly, potatoes, green salad too
Will have your guests asking for more.

So why would you pardon a turkey?
Did he do some serious wrong?
NO! Honor the guy for his great sacrifice
And he'll burst into turkey song.

The turkey should pardon the office
The president represents.
Really, to pardon a turkey
Simply doesn't make any sense

The Dinosaur

In swampy days of long ago
Strange creatures walked on earth.
Some were great big dinosaurs.
They were even large at birth.

More and more the dinosaurs
Ate everything in sight.
Their bodies grew enormous
As they devoured each bite.

So they could reach the food up high
Their necks grew even taller
To support small heads that did not think
As their brain grew even smaller.

They did not plan for others.
They did not think ahead.
They lived only in the moment.
Now all dinosaurs are dead.

Though they now lie in pools of oil
We think of them as power.
They are a source of energy
We've set out to devour.

Could this be what the future holds
As we gorge our appetites
And exploit the scarce resources
For which mankind now fights?

If we don't plan for posterity
Will mankind fade away?
Will our power in the future
Be like the Dinosaur's today?

When you are 92 years old and you are just sitting there, this kind of silly thing sometimes happens. Sorry about that Mr. Poe

Raven, Beware of Overquothing

Once upon an early morning, sun was rising on a Bore—
Stupid Raven quothing like he never had before.

Perching on a vaulted barn door waking chickens from their snore
Raven just kept on quothing. He was filled with quoths galore.

Other Ravens round about him had a quoth or two to share
But he wouldn't listen to them.. For their thoughts he did not care.

In the middle of his quothing someone shouted "cut it out!
Quit your quothing Stupid Raven, no one cares what it's about".

Stupid Raven was not daunted; he just quothed a whole lot more.
Someone threw a corn cob at him and it knocked him to the floor.

As he lay there writhing, kicking, while his raven feathers flew
It suddenly occurred to him: his quothing days were through.

His final quoth before he choked was
"I'm sorry!"

There's a moral to this story just before this poem ends
"Share the air in conversation when you are visiting with friends".

228

"Only God Can Make A Tree"
He Leaves The Pruning Up To Me

In appreciation to the flower committee

When you enter the commons at Morningside,
Among the first things you'll see there
Are stunning arrangements of nature's gifts
Selected and placed there with care.

Some are flowers and leaves from our gardens
That so often are passed by unseen
As we hasten to do all the things we must do
And take a few naps in between.

There are sensitive creative people
Who see beauty in each flower a tree
And who love to bring them together
Sharing visions for you and for me

To accent the gifts from God's gardens,
They choose each container or vase
To frame and project the beauty
The creator provided with grace.

We thank you for sharing your talents,
We thank you for following through.
Though he provides us generous blessings,
God doesn't do the part you do.

For Our Wedding Day

My dear I am sure it was ever thus
You and I, each alone,
Would some day be us.
As we stand here together declaring our love
We are grateful for guidance
That comes from above

On our separate journeys from long ago
It is probably good
That each did not know
That somewhere the other was on the way
To this cherished moment
-Our wedding day!

We first needed time to become
Who we are
As we searched for the meaning of life
You became you and I became me
And tonight
We've become man and wife.

As we moved towards each other
From separate stars.
We've gathered friends by the way
We are honored and thrilled
That they are here
To share in our wonderful day.

Now that our journey begins as one
We can share joys and sorrows
And worlds of fun
Someday when we dangle our kids on our knees
And remember this glorious day
Someone may ask "Would you change anything?"

Together we'll shout out, "No way!"

230

The Croquet Game

I watched a croquet game today.
As I sat in the shade of the trees surrounding the court,
Now and then a few waves of guilt swept through me,
Feelings that perhaps I should be attending to
"matters of consequence".....finishing a
project...beginning a project...
Accomplish something!

The game brought about memories of another year...
In the secluded hills and valleys of the Rocky Mountains
Where on Sunday afternoons, between those days of rest,
Men and women, boys and girls, tossed off
The cares of the hard labor required of life in the country
To play together... to challenge one another in
Games... the favorite being, croquet.

A light breeze rustled leaves,
Quiet voices gave advice the players could not hear.
The competition was between two women.
Women don't tell their ages, but neither was younger
than 80.
Sunshine washed the court where they played
In the presence of balding men and white-haired women
Entitled to sit on the sidelines and make their mental
suggestions
Of how each player could have made a better decision.

These people had traveled through depression and wars,
Through monumental social and economic changes,
Through political upheavals,
Through scandals in the Church,
Through family support and disagreements
Through conquering of the enslaving's of sickness
Through joys and sorrows of births and deaths.

As if breaking the sound barrier
They had come through all the trials and tribulations of
living
To enjoy the beauty of springtime…. the freedom from
responsibility,
To play croquet.
And that's o.k.

Made in the USA
Monee, IL
07 July 2026

56551547R00134